SPITFIRE

THE BIOGRAPHY

JONATHAN GLANCEY

Atlantic Books
London

8 9

A CIP catalogue record for this book is available from the British Library.

ISBN 978 1 84354 528 6

All technical drawings by Mark Rolfe © Mark Rolfe Technical Art

Printed in Great Britain by Clays Ltd, St Ives plc

Atlantic Books
An imprint of Grove Atlantic Ltd
Ormond House
26–27 Boswell Street
London WC1N 3JZ

SPITFIRE

Jonathan Glancey is the architecture and design editor of the *Guardian*. He is also a pilot and a frequent broadcaster. His books include *The Story of Architecture* and *The Train: an illustrated history*.

'This account has an immediacy that does justice to the fighting, and the fighter.' Derek Robinson, *Guardian*

'Jonathan Glancey, full of boyish affection for his subject, has delivered an enthusiastic and energetic account of what is still the world's most famous marque of aeroplane.' Jon Latimer, *TLS*

'A passionate, personal, anecdotal and technically literate biography of the enduringly symbolic British fighting aircraft, the Spitfire.' Iain Finlayson, *Saga*

'A treat. Stylishly written and entertainingly told, *Spitfire* is a real treasure-trove of fascinating anecdotes and little-known facts that gets to the heart of our love affair with the Spitfire. A wonderful book.' Rowland White

'At last – a book about the Spitfire that is not just for aficionados. Full of wonderful anecdotes and hugely entertaining, *Spitfire* is told with the passion and style that this most iconic of aircraft deserves.' James Holland

'The Supermarine Spitfire holds a very special place in British hearts. Jonathan Glancey's biography of this machine – which is at the same time a history of aviation, of design, of the war in the air, of the people who made the Spitfire, of national fictions since then, as well as being the story of a man who grew up reading about Paddy Payne fighter pilot in the *Lion* comic – at last does justice to a remarkable story, and does it stylishly as well.' Christopher Frayling

I can hardly better the dedication Alfred Price made in his excellent *Spitfire: A Complete Fighting History* 'to the men and women who transposed the Spitfire – a mere fabrication of aluminium alloy, steel, rubber, Perspex and a few other things – into the centrepiece of an epic without parallel in the history of aviation'.

Nonetheless, I would like to add my own – to the infamous memory of Britain's New Labour governments, their love of ill-founded war and their authoritarian fight, undertaken with greater effectiveness than the Luftwaffe, to undermine those civil liberties and hard-won traditions of freedom fought for by decent people over many centuries, and especially by those, of whatever nationality, class, creed, colour, age, gender or political affiliation, who designed, built and flew the Spitfire.

And in loving memory of my father.

CONTENTS

LIST OF ILLUSTRATIONS

SPITFIRE

INTRODUCTION

'IT'S the sort of bloody silly name they would give it.' R. J. Mitchell, inventor of the Spitfire, the most famous, best-loved and most beautiful of all fighter aircraft, was not exactly impressed by the tricksy appellation some cove flying a desk in Whitehall is said to have come up with for his prototype Supermarine Type 300 monoplane. The aircraft answering to Air Ministry specification F.37/34 had, in fact, been named by Sir Robert McClean, chairman of Vickers, the company that had bought the Supermarine Aviation Works, after his young daughter Anna, a right little 'spitfire'. As for Merlin, the name given to the magnificent 1,000-hp Rolls-Royce V12 aero-engine that powered the Spitfire, this had been a wonderfully apt choice by Rolls-Royce itself. The Merlin proved to be the stuff of mechanical wizardry and, as the loudly beating heart of the stunning little fighter aircraft that soared into British skies against Hitler's Luftwaffe in 1940, it was a significant part of the spell, and more than a flash of the sorcery, that led to the Nazis' *Götterdämmerung* in 1945.

Rolls-Royce had actually named what was to become its most famous aero-engine not after the Arthurian wizard but after the falcon the Americans know, rather prosaically, as the pigeon hawk, and the British, more poetically, as the merlin. Rolls-Royce had a policy of naming its engines after birds of prey – the Eagle, Kestrel, Peregrine, Griffon and Vulture were all installed with varying degrees of success in RAF aircraft. The Merlin, though, was a perfect match from the very start for Mitchell's promising little fighter. The avian merlin is a raptor with thin, pointed wings that allow it to dive at sensational speed. The Spitfire's famously thin wing enabled it too to dive at very great speeds, so much so that in 1943 one of Mitchell's sensational machines was not so very far from breaking the sound barrier. Not that a piston-engined aircraft ever has achieved this; it took the custom-designed and rocket-powered Bell X-1, 'Glamorous Glennis', to do the job in October 1947 with Captain Charles 'Chuck' Yeager at the controls. During the Second World War, Yeager had flown the North American P-51D Mustang,

A restored Spitfire Mk I rolls above the Seven Sisters Cliffs, Friston, West Sussex, in 1988.

a superb American fighter powered by a Rolls-Royce Merlin, built under licence by Packard in Detroit. It was also the stuff of aero-industrial sorcery.

The fastest falcon of all, the peregrine, can reach a speed of up to around 200 mph in a headlong dive in pursuit of its prey. The Victorian Jesuit priest Gerard Manley Hopkins evoked the flight of one of these mercurial raptors in an exhilarating, tongue-tripping poem, 'The Windhover':

> I caught this morning morning's minion, king-
>   dom of daylight's dauphin, dapple-dawn-drawn Falcon, in his riding
>   Of the rolling level underneath him steady air, and striding
> High there, how he rung upon the rein of a wimpling wing
> In his ecstasy! then off, off forth on swing,
>   As a skate's heel sweeps smooth on a bow-bend: the hurl and gliding
>   Rebuffed the big wind. My heart in hiding
> Stirred for a bird, – the achieve of, the mastery of the thing!

When I first read those words, dedicated by the poet to 'Christ Our Lord', I was a schoolboy at what I thought of as a Catholic Stalag Luft. I was fascinated by birds and in love with aircraft and the idea of flight, and I thought of Hopkins's falcon as a Spitfire scything through the air, 'off forth on swing as a skate's heel sweeps smooth on a bow-bend'. It was as if Hopkins had actually seen a Spitfire, another kind of saviour, in flight – although if he had, he would surely have described the sound of the Merlin engine that accompanies the flight of this most dangerously exquisite mechanical bird of prey. The Merlin's voice is all thunder and lightning, a deep, pulsing roar overlain with the throaty whistle of its supercharger.

'Rumble thy bellyful! Spit, fire! spout, rain!' Even in this line from Shakespeare's *King Lear* (Act 3, scene 2) that I happened to alight upon at much the same time as I flew on mind's wings with Hopkins's falcon, I could hear the basso profundo thrum of a Merlin and the blazing sight and chattering sound of Browning .303 machine-guns, or the pom-pom thud of Hispano 20-mm cannon, raining revenge from the wings of a fighter that really did spit fire.

Of course, for any English schoolboy of my generation who could assemble 1/72 scale Airfix Spitfires – a squadron of them, in fact, lovingly painted and detailed, complete with oil leaks from their glossy black Merlins – and do so without spreading strands of Britfix 77 glue and telltale fingerprints across their Lilliputian windscreens, there was another poem, that those who loved aircraft, yet pretended not to care a fig for literature, knew by heart:

Oh! I have slipped the surly bonds of earth
And danced the skies on laughter-silvered wings;
Sunward I've climbed, and joined the tumbling mirth
Of sun-split clouds – and done a hundred things
You have not dreamed of – wheeled and soared and swung
High in the sunlit silence. Hov'ring there
I've chased the shouting wind along, and flung
My eager craft through footless halls of air.
Up, up the long delirious, burning blue,
I've topped the windswept heights with easy grace
Where never lark, or even eagle flew –
And, while with silent, lifting mind I've trod
The high untrespassed sanctity of space,
Put out my hand and touched the face of God.

4

In this poem, 'High Flight', the flight of the Spitfire is rhapsodically evoked. It was written by Pilot Officer John Gillespie Magee Jr, an American Spitfire pilot, born in Shanghai, who crossed the Canadian border illegally in 1941, while still a freshman at Yale, to serve with the Royal Canadian Air Force in England. 'An aeroplane,' he wrote home while undergoing basic training in Canada, 'is not to us a weapon of war, but a flash of silver slanting the skies; the hum of a deep-voiced motor; a feeling of dizziness; it is speed and ecstasy.' Of his flying, his instructor noted, 'Patches of brilliance; tendency to over-confidence.'

Magee flew a Spitfire Mk V with the RCAF's 412 Squadron from Dibgy, Lincolnshire, from 30 June 1941. In early September, he wrote to his parents, after a high-altitude test flight, 'I am enclosing a verse I wrote the other day. It started at 30,000 feet, and was finished soon after I landed. I thought it might interest you.' On the back of the letter was 'High Flight', written on 3 September, exactly two years after Great Britain had declared war on Germany. On 11 December 1941, three days after the United States entered the war, Magee was killed in a flying accident close to RAF Tangmere. A farmer saw his Spitfire drop from the sky, and watched as Magee bailed out. His parachute failed to open. His grave is in the quiet churchyard of Holy Cross, Scopwick, Lincolnshire. In icily precise lettering, a white military tombstone reminds us that he was just nineteen years old.

'The Windhover', Lear raving, Magee's 'High Flight': these loops and rolls of words all fuse and fly together in the delirious blue of the imagination to shape a portrait of the Spitfire, a winged minion of death chevying on air-built thoroughfares, one of the finest aircraft yet designed. A man of matter-of-fact sensibilities, Mitchell himself would have turned on his heel and walked out of the drawing shop rather than listen to any of this florid, literary hyperbole; yet the Spitfire was a brilliant name, at once lyrical and charismatic. Deadly accurate, too.

Mitchell preferred the name 'Shrew', which proves that perhaps he really did have no ear for poetry. Supermarine Shrew sounds plain wrong, even though in Elizabethan England shrill and shrewish women were often called 'spitfires'. The shrew itself is a truly voracious predator – but short-lived. The pygmy shrew, the fiercest of the breed, burns itself up in an orgy of hunting to stay alive; it rarely soldiers on beyond fifteen months before giving up its tiny ghost. Many Spitfires, along with their young and inexperienced pilots, were destroyed within a day or two of going into battle. The record went to a Spitfire Mk I, X4110, which was delivered to 602 Squadron, West Hampnett, near Chichester, on 18 August 1940: within two hours it was being flown in anger by Flight Lieutenant J. Dunlop-Urie and jumped by Messerschmitt Bf 109s. Dunlop-Urie survived a crash landing; X4110 was written off. Very few Spitfires were to survive all six years of the Second World War. Those that did included the very first delivered to an RAF squadron in 1938. Yet even when short-lived, a Spitfire was always more than a shrew.

I cannot remember a time when Spitfires did not play some part in my life. My Uncle Jack, a Wellington man – bomber, not school – was shot down and killed over Klagenfurt, Austria, in 1944, flying on a mission with 70 Squadron from Foggia on the Adriatic coast of Italy. My father had clearly loved his younger brother and so, I suppose, this was in part why he, like so many others who had friends and relatives killed in the Second World War, was not particularly keen to talk about combat. My father's blue RAF jacket hung in the furthest recesses of a capacious bedroom wardrobe. His medals, a little tarnished, lay unceremoniously in a pewter cigarette box. In my parents' bedroom, there was a lovely wedding portrait of them, taken in 1940 – my father in uniform, my mother with an RAF wing brooch pinning the top of her blouse. There were battered, green-painted steel models of Spitfires and Hurricanes, and of enemy fighters and bombers, used for identification and training purposes, in a dark and cobwebbed shoe-cupboard. The only tales my father liked to tell of those days of cordite, oxygen and ethylene glycol were of his times towards the end of the war in the jungles of Burma, and in the Naga Hills, of the writhing body of a poisonous snake he mistook for a shower-hose when he had suds rather than the sun in his eyes, or of how beautiful the Buddhist temples of Rangoon were. I liked

The author's mother and father, then an officer cadet, at the time of their engagement.

the silk pilot's maps he would have carried in a pocket, and the guide to surviving a crash in the jungle. The advice on what to do if he had met a tiger was nicely to the point: pray.

There were dog-eared boxes on a shelf at the top of a cupboard stuffed with wonderfully crisp black-and-white reconnaissance photographs, taken at little more than tree height from the noses of Beaufighters and the bellies of Spitfires. Many featured temples, not because these were potential RAF targets, but because they acted as turning points for aircraft and, I like to think, simply because they were beautiful to look at, as if someone, centuries ago, had decided to turn the sun into architecture. So, although as a boy I walked stiff-legged behind Douglas Bader, who found this funny, although I knew my Stalags and my Spitfires inside out – even the firing order of the Merlin's twelve cylinders, starting with 1A, followed by 6B and ending with 2B after 5A – although I had mastered every last detail of all the fighter aircraft that flew in the Second World War, although I had devoured Guy Gibson's *Enemy Coast Ahead*, Pierre Clostermann's *The Big Show*, P. R. Reid's *Escape from Colditz*, *The Cockleshell Heroes* by C. E. Lucas Phillips, and countless other wartime epics, I was to remain frustrated, all too aware that fighting talk among the adults I knew was taboo. Combat could only be exercised in black tar playgrounds when we played British vs Germans and Spitfires vs Messerschmitts, coming in to land, after furious, dakka-dakka machine-gun fire, only when the school bell clanged and we were grounded by arithmetic, spelling, rulers across the backs of legs and religious instruction.

My Uncle Reg, a major blown up in Libya on service with the Eighth Army and with a hole in his head you could place your index finger in, told me that only those who 'fought from the cookhouse' banged on about 'action' – and killing. In RAF terminology, he meant those who 'flew desks'. None of this matters much; what does matter is that, although I adored Spitfires from primary school age, I never really thought of what it must have been like to have killed in one, even though I must have drawn hundreds of Spitfires blazing away at Stukas and Messerschmitts on the pages of my school exercise books; nor what it would have been like to have had someone trying to kill me.

The mortal reality of aerial combat remained the stuff of boys' comics read on floors, among a tangle of dogs, head held in cupped hands. There was Paddy Payne, Warrior of the Skies, in the *Lion*. I pored over his adventures even before I could read. The scripts, I learned much later on, were by a chap called Mark Ross; they were chock-full of classic wartime comic-book phrases such as 'Achtung! Spitfeur!', 'Teufel!', 'For you, Herr Payne, the war is over', 'Cop a load of this, Fritz' and 'Ach! The fortunes of war', along with a hamperful of 'goshes' and 'crikeys' amid guttural, sausage-eating exclamations of 'Gott im Himmel!' and 'Donner und Blitzen!'. As for the drawings, by Joe Colquhoun, who had also drawn the original 'Roy of the Rovers' strips in the *Tiger*, these were both accurate and exciting. They included, as best I can remember, various marks of Spitfires, including Fleet Air Arm Seafires and, rather surprisingly, Spitfire floatplanes, only a handful of which were ever built. They even had Squadron Leader Payne threatened by such Nazi exotica as the Bachem Ba 349 Natter (Viper), a tiny rocket-powered inter-ceptor that was meant, in theory, to have shot up into formations of Allied bombers at a truly astonishing rate of climb. It let loose its twenty-four rockets, and then rammed one of the enemy aircraft in a final gesture of defiance as the pilot ejected his way to safety in what little remained of Nazi Germany in the spring of 1945.

Paddy Payne, of course, gave the Natter short shrift in what, I suppose, must have been a late-model, Griffon-engined Spitfire. Payne's Second World War was to continue for thirteen years in the pages of the *Lion* – more than twice as long as the real war and far longer than my interest in reading his adventures. In that time, he must have shot down pretty much the entire Luftwaffe. No wonder the Germans of the liberal and democratic Bundesrepublik were upset; no wonder they said the British were still obsessed by the war.

As I grew up, so my love for the Spitfire evolved, just as the machine itself was to do between 1936 and 1947. As I spread my wings, so the Spitfire flew with me. When I first went to France as a schoolboy, now in love with architecture of every era, and under my own steam – in fact, on the last of the Chapelon Pacific locomotives running from Calais Maritime to Abbeville on the way to Paris – a Spitfire Mk IX flew overhead. The sight encouraged me to read again the memoirs of the French ace Pierre Clostermann (thirty-three kills claimed), this time, haltingly, in the original. Years later, when I travelled as a student to India, to Burma, the Naga Hills and beyond, I met men who had flown or serviced Spitfires. When I first went to see the extraordinary concrete architecture created by Le Corbusier in Chandigarh, the new capital of East Punjab, I found a Spitfire Mk XVIII in retirement at the local Punjab Engineering College. Later still, I learned to fly and eventually progressed from Tiger Moths to the cockpit of a Spitfire Mk VIII. I cannot really add anything to the praise that has been heaped upon the Spitfire; it is truly an aircraft the pilot wears like a second skin. I have driven many fine sports cars of all periods, yet none comes remotely close to the precision of a Spitfire. It scythes through the air like the sharpest imaginable blade. It pulls on the heartstrings even as it concentrates the mind. It is a mechanical spirit of ecstasy, the very sensation of flight.

Now, as the father of a young daughter, I have kept myself, temporarily at least, closer to the ground than I have for a long while. And yet the Spitfire stays with me. What I have learned in recent years is sketched through the pages of this book. When I was a small boy, I thought that the Spitfire was flown exclusively by decent British chaps of my father's generation and social set, men who drove wire-wheeled MGs with black labradors in the passenger seat, along with a few plucky Poles thrown in for good measure. Since then, I have learned that Spitfires were flown by both men and women, not just from across Britain, its Commonwealth and Empire, but by Czechs, Russians and Americans too. Indian Sikhs in turbans flew them. Black West Indians. A Navajo Indian. After the Second World War, rival Spitfires were flown in anger by Israelis, Syrians and Egyptians. French Spitfire pilots strafed guerrillas in French Indo-China; RAF Spitfire pilots did the same in Malaysia.

Spitfires flew under the flags of many nations: Australia, Belgium, Burma, Canada, the People's Republic of China, Czechoslovakia, Denmark, Egypt, France, Greece, Holland, India, Ireland, Israel, Italy, New Zealand, Norway, Portugal, the Soviet Union, South Africa, Southern Rhodesia, Sweden, Syria, Thailand, Turkey, the United States and Yugoslavia. Perhaps fittingly, the last time a Spitfire flew in military service was in England in 1963, when a Mk XIX, the fastest of all the Spitfire marks, was pitted in a mock dog-fight against a frontline RAF Lightning jet-fighter capable of Mach 2. It had seemed possible at the time that the Lightning might be sent to Indonesia, where it would fly against P-51D Mustangs. The RAF felt that its fighter pilots needed to know what it might be like if they came up against one of these still potent Second World War veterans. The Spitfire was the nearest thing the RAF had to a Mustang. It acquitted itself remarkably well.

I have talked to those involved with the Spitfire in one way or another over the course of four decades. I think I know enough about the aircraft themselves (although any corrections to this book, which cannot pretend to be definitive, are welcome), and yet there is always more to learn about the men and women who together wove the tale of this magnificent machine. This, in any case, is really their story, not mine. And, of course, the story of that remarkable fabrication of aluminium alloy, steel, rubber and Perspex.

CHAPTER I

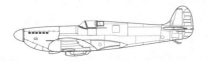

OF MONOPLANES
AND MEN

W AS the Spitfire a work of art? It is a perennially fascinating question, even if of little interest to military experts or historians, and its answer is inseparable from the neverending debate as to which was the better fighter, the Spitfire or the Messerschmitt Bf 109. The Bf 109, some would claim, was the superior wartime machine because it was easier, and so cheaper, to build than the Spitfire. A kit of parts that slotted and bolted together in precise, factory-like fashion, the German fighter was also simpler to service and maintain. It was, therefore, the more truly industrial machine – not so elegantly formed or finely crafted as the British Spitfire, but an instrument of death better suited, perhaps, to a machine-age war in which command of the air was essential to victory. In fact, the Spitfire's unstated artistry counted against it.

As it was, both aircraft were developed and manufactured throughout the Second World War: altogether, some 31,000 Bf 109s were built and some 22,000 Spitfires. Both were highly successful, but in the end the RAF was on the winning side and so the argument was always going to be academic. In reality, there had not been much between the performance of these rival fighters, although development of the Bf 109 finally tailed off as the Allies squeezed into submission both Nazi Germany and what had been, until remarkably late in the conflict, its astonishingly productive war machine, driven by the architect-turned-armaments minister Albert Speer. As much as anything else, it was the quality of pilots that made the difference.

A Spitfire was a superb fighter, but even some of its best pilots, from a purely aeronautic point of view, were poor shots and so unable to make the most effective use of this finely honed weapon of war. The top-ranking Spitfire pilot measured in terms of number of kills made during the Second World War was Johnnie Johnson, who shot down thirty-eight enemy aircraft. The leading Luftwaffe aces, with most of their kills made through the gunsights of Bf 109s, were Erich Hartmann (352), Gerhard Barkhorn (301) and Gunther Rall (275). Despite this huge discrepancy between the scores of British and German aces, this did not reflect on the relative efficacy of their aircraft. Where RAF pilots were recalled for rest, training and fresh assignments, their Luftwaffe counterparts were expected to fly until they died, or the war was won. They also flew, especially in the first two years of the Russian campaign, against an inexperienced enemy yet to be equipped with either the commanders it needed or the right sort of aircraft. Flying against the RAF was a very different proposition, although even then German aces ruled the roost until well into the Battle of Britain.

Spitfire and Messerschmitt were certainly products of two very different industrial cultures. Where the Bf 109 was undoubtedly a practical, economical and workmanlike piece of design, the Spitfire emerged from a culture famous for producing lithe, good-looking and even sensual machinery. The Spitfire, then, was a thing of complex compound curves, of wings blended gracefully into a smoothly lined fuselage requiring a great deal of hand-finishing. In fact, the Spitfire was considered to be so difficult and expensive to build that the Air Ministry very nearly cancelled orders for it as late as May 1940. But the Spitfire flew as beautifully as its catwalk looks suggested it would. Its elegant elliptical wings – which meant that, in general, it could be mistaken for no other aircraft – may well have been expensive and tricky to make, yet their slim and effectively swept-back profile enabled the aircraft to turn tight circles and, as engines became ever more powerful, to dive and to fly still faster and to meet the ever-increasing demands of the war in the air.

Ultimately, the Spitfire proved capable of further development than the Bf 109, and it continued into production well into 1947. The very last Spitfire to be produced – the F 24 – weighed half as much again as the first machines, could climb twice as quickly, had a top speed 25 per cent higher and could pack a much greater punch with its four 20-mm cannon and, if required, rockets and 500-lb bombs. These end-of-line Spitfires are fine-looking machines, although they are clearly tougher and less overtly crafted or, dare I say it, artistic than either Mitchell's prototype or the Battle of Britain's legendary Mk Is.

Mitchell, of course, would have dismissed any reference to art or artistry in the design of the Spitfire as stuff and nonsense. He saw himself as an entirely practical fellow, and the aesthetic of his fighter purely the product of the functional requirements, mathematics and aerodynamics that governed its form. Beverley Shenstone, the young Canadian aerodynamicist who worked closely with Mitchell on the design of the prototype, recalled: 'I once remember discussing the wing shape with him, and he said, jokingly, "I don't give a bugger whether it's elliptical or not, so long as it covers the guns.'"

Did Mitchell protest too much? At school he had been good at art, while his younger brother Billy was very good indeed. Billy set up his own business designing patterns for Royal Crown Derby, Minton, Spode and other leading companies in the English ceramic industry centred on Stoke-on-Trent. Stoke had been one of the crucibles of the Industrial Revolution, and it was where art and industry were fused together for the first time to create what was known as industrial art and what we know as industrial, or product, design.

Reginald Joseph Mitchell was brought up in a world of art, artistry, machines and smoking chimneys. One of five children, he was born on 20 May 1895 at 115 Congleton Road, Butt Lane, near Stoke-on-Trent, in a house flanking what is now the busy A34 trunk road. The Reginald Mitchell Primary School is just down the road from Number 115. Reginald's parents, Herbert Mitchell, a Yorkshireman, and Elizabeth Brain, were both successful and well-respected teachers. Herbert later set up a printing business and the family moved to 87 Chaplin Road, Normacott, a terraced house in a suburb of Longton. Today, the ground floor is home to Tony's hairdressing salon.

Mitchell was already making model gliders from strips of wood and glued paper when the Wright Brothers made their first powered flight from Kitty Hawk, North Carolina, in 1903. He was gripped by the idea of flight and yet when he left Hanley High School he began an engineering apprenticeship with Kerr Stuart, a local firm of locomotive builders that had moved from Glasgow to Stoke-on-Trent in 1892. In some ways, Kerr Stuart seemed an odd choice for a young man with a flair for art as well as maths; the locomotives made by the company were prosaic machines built to standard designs and sold 'off the shelf', mostly to narrow-gauge railways around the world. Some, like the 'Wren' 0-4-0 saddle tank, were very small indeed, weighing less than Stephenson's Rocket of 1829, and few Kerr Stuart locomotives would have been much, if at all, faster than that famous Regency flyer. Examples of the kind of Kerr Stuart locomotives Mitchell would have been familiar with can be seen working today on narrow-gauge railways including the Talyllyn in North Wales, the Great Whipsnade Railway at the Bedfordshire zoo, and the Sandstone Steam Railway in South Africa. Modest machines, they have nevertheless travelled as extensively as Spitfires, if rather more slowly.

If Mitchell had been apprenticed to the nearby Stoke locomotive works of the North Staffordshire Railway, his path might well have crossed that of Tom Coleman, another highly practical engineer with excellent maths and an artistic bent, the latter something he, too, would vigorously deny all his life. It is to Coleman we owe the splendid 'Princess Coronation'-class Pacifics of 1937, designed under the direction of William Stanier, Chief Mechanical Engineer of the London Midland and Scottish Railway. Stanier was away inspecting locomotives in India during the genesis of these magnificent machines, yet they were to prove the most powerful (3,333 ihp) and, at 114 mph, the second-fastest class of British steam locomotives on record. They combined a restrained beauty and nobility of line that was very much down to Coleman, who was also directly responsible for their heroic performance, economic working, reliability and popularity among crews, maintenance staff, railway management and travelling public alike. Like Mitchell, Coleman was an essentially shy and self-effacing chap, a team player in an enterprise he always saw as much bigger than himself.

I mention Coleman because he came from the same social and engineering culture as Mitchell. These were men who knew, as if by instinct, how to draw a beautiful line, but would have denied that their machines were works of art in any sense, not even accidentally. And yet both achieved feats of engineering design that were to stir hearts and imaginations. They are, too, a part of the same breed as those who went on to design such exquisitely beautiful machines as Concorde; official research on the development of a revolutionary supersonic airliner began just two years after the last, subsonic, piston-engined Spitfire retired from regular duties with the RAF in 1954, and indeed the Spitfire had played its part in some of the earliest research into supersonic flight.

Although it is easier to imagine the young Mitchell at work on the design of high-speed railway flyers rather than narrow-gauge plodders, the lightness of Kerr Stuart locomotives may well have appealed to him; in any case, his sights were set high above narrow-gauge rails and very firmly on aircraft, and flight. While working in the drawing office at Kerr Stuart, he pursued a higher education, studying engineering, mechanics and advanced mathematics at night school. At home, he used what spare time he had to work at his own lathe in an effort to master practical engineering skills.

Mitchell's industry paid off. At the age of just twenty-two, he was taken on at the Supermarine Aviation Works. This had been founded on the site of a former coal wharf on the River Itchen at Woolston, Southampton, in 1913 by Noel Pemberton-Billing, a yacht dealer, and his friend Hubert Scott-Paine, to build seaplanes. Pemberton-Billing was a racy character. He lived on his three-masted schooner moored in the Itchen. Of the money he put up to found Supermarine, £500 had come from a wager; Pemberton-Billing had bet that he could gain his Royal Aero Club certificate, or flying licence, within twenty-four hours of first sitting at the controls of an aircraft. He won. In 1914, as a reserve officer in the Navy, he helped to organize a daring bombing raid by British naval aircraft on German Zeppelin sheds on the shore of Lake Constance. Pemberton-Billing was elected a Member of Parliament, and to avoid a clash of interests with his business affairs – something hard to imagine today – he handed Supermarine over to the equally restless Scott-Paine.

It was Scott-Paine who hired Mitchell, and Scott-Paine who was to get Supermarine involved in the famous Schneider Trophy air races. He moved on, in the mid-1920s, to form British Power Boats, where he was to design and build the highly successful Type 2 HSL air-sea rescue boats, first launched in 1937. 'Flown' by RAF crew, these 63-foot boats were powered by Napier Sea Lion aero-engines and had a top speed of thirty-six knots. They served with distinction throughout the Second World War and were used in the first British Commando raids against naval targets in German-occupied France. Spitfire pilots would have every reason to be grateful to Scott-Paine. In hiring Mitchell, he got them up into the air; by producing the Type 2 HSL, he brought them home safely when they fell from the sky, and into the drink.

Within three years of arriving in Southampton, and by now married to Florence Dayson, a headmistress from back home in Stoke, Mitchell, or 'RJ' as he was known at Supermarine, became the company's Chief Engineer. Between 1920 and 1936 he designed twenty-four different machines ranging from light aircraft and fighters to huge flying boats and bombers. Not all of these went into production, but they show the range of his aerial ambition, and the depths of his skill as a designer. With this prodigious and prolific talent at the drawing board, Supermarine was to remain profitable throughout the great economic depression that was to sink so many businesses in the years following the Wall Street Crash of 1929.

Mitchell's genius as a designer and engineer was to think for himself, in his own time, while listening to everyone around him. He would not have fitted easily into the structure of a modern company where crushingly boring meetings, inane management jargon, market research, focus groups and corporate culture are all-important. He was, in any case, rather shy, with a bit of a stammer, and, perhaps as a result, notoriously blunt. He needed time by himself for thinking, walking, sailing, shooting or playing golf, or just sitting in a deckchair listening to birds sing in his garden. Although he was one of those men of whom obituaries say 'he did not suffer fools gladly', Mitchell – 'Mitch' to his test pilots – was respectful and loyal. He gave talented colleagues their head. He listened intently to what the most junior fitter had to say. And he said a most emphatic 'No' to Vickers Aviation (Vickers-Armstrong from 1938), the company that bought out Supermarine in 1928, when it tried to foist its own chief designer on his team. That designer was Barnes Wallis, who went on to shape the Vickers Wellington bomber, invent the bouncing bomb of Dambusters fame and, later, to pioneer the swing-wing technology that produced the distinctive supersonic F-111 bomber for the United States Air Force in 1967. That Mitchell could dismiss such obvious talent, and get away with it, says much about both the quiet force of his personality, and how highly he was regarded by the desk-jockeys of the mighty Vickers corporation.

R. J. Mitchell at a Schneider Cup dinner in Southampton in 1931.

Many of his more prosaic aircraft might surprise those who know Mitchell only for the Spitfire. The highly successful Supermarine Southampton and Stranraer flying boats were, for example, very much workaday machines. Rather ungainly-looking biplanes, they flew low, slowly and well, around the world. The Southampton, rather resembling a survivor drawn from the embers of the First World War, flew with the RAF from 1925 to 1936, while its successor, the only slightly sleeker Stranraer, performed with the RAF and RCAF throughout the Second World War. My great aunt Flo and her gun-toting mercenary partner Mervin, who had shot his, and her, way out of Japanese-occupied Singapore and who settled in Vancouver after the Second World War, recalled flying Queen Charlotte Airlines' Stranraers along the coast of British Columbia.

These flying boats represent one very important aspect of Mitchell's work: safety. He was one of the very few aircraft designers who learned to fly, and this showed in the way his aircraft handled both on the ground and in the sky. Fast and deadly though it was, a Spitfire was a very safe aircraft to fly – and easy too. Many Second World War pilots were to be grateful to Mitchell, not just for the Spitfire they chased the enemy with, but also for his tough little Supermarine Walrus amphibian, first flown in 1936; one of these would often be there to rescue them when they were forced to bail out over water or ditch into the sea. Walrus biplanes flew, with their top speed of just 145 mph at 4,750 feet, trouble-free throughout the Second World War. Even the Walrus, though, could be flown with surprising brio. Flight Lieutenant George Pickering, Supermarine's test pilot, made a point of looping the loop in new Walruses floated out from the factory. He liked to start his loops from as low as 300 feet: Mitchell, with a little help from his pilots, was truly a wizard of flight.

He was also fascinated by speed, and especially so through Supermarine's involvement in the Schneider Trophy, a glamorous prize for the world's fastest seaplanes, founded in 1912 by Jacques Schneider, a wealthy French aviation enthusiast. The aim, with an initial bait of £1,000 for the winning team, was to encourage progress in civil aviation, but the event soon became an out-and-out race and a quest for sheer speed between rival nations whose governments learned to back manufacturers as they realized the potential spin-off for the design of future military aircraft. Schneider's rules stated that if any nation won the race three times in a row, it would keep the trophy in perpetuity.

France was the winner of the first Schneider race, held at Monaco in 1913 over a triangular course measuring 174 miles. Flying a Deperdussin monoplane equipped with a 160-hp Gnome rotary engine, Maurice Prévost completed his best circuit of the course at an average of 45.75 mph. Great Britain won, at Monaco again, the following year, with C. Howard Pixton whizzing a 100-hp Gnome-engined Sopwith Tabloid around the circuit at 86.8 mph. Then the First World War intervened. Supermarine, along with fellow British manufacturers Sopwith, Fairey and Avro, entered the first post-war race, held in Bournemouth in 1919, but the Sea Lion of Squadron Leader Basil Hobbs foundered with a hole in its hull after he had landed earlier to check his bearings and hit a wreck while taking off again. The poor organisation of the event led to protests, however, and the Italians were only declared the winners two weeks later. Their consolation was to host the next race, in Venice in 1920. The Italians duly won, with a Savoia managing 106.7 mph, and did so again in 1921, with a Macchi aircraft averaging 111 mph over a slightly different course at the same venue. Italy was favourite to win again in 1922 in Naples. This was the year that Mussolini marched on Rome and established his Fascist state, and it would have been a black eye for Europe's liberal democracies if the Fascists had succeeded in making off with the Schneider Trophy for good. In the event, Supermarine checked the Italians' ambition with a win by Captain

H. C. Biard, flying Mitchell's privately funded Sea Lion II biplane powered by a 456-hp Napier engine at 145.7 mph.

The event was by now hugely popular, drawing seaside crowds of up to a quarter of a million. The Americans won at Cowes in 1923, at 177.38 mph. The 1924 race was cancelled. The Americans won again in 1925, when Lieutenant James H. Doolittle did very much indeed by flitting around the prescribed circuit at Chesapeake Bay, Baltimore, in a 620-hp Curtiss R3C-2 biplane at no less than 232.57 mph. This was the same Jimmy Doolittle, a pilot veteran of the First World War, who was to lead the first, and much celebrated, carrier-based bomber attack on mainland Japan in 1942. The British entry, Mitchell's stunning, streamlined S 4 monoplane, crashed. Its pilot, Captain Biard, was pulled alive from the wreckage. The cause of the crash was never established, although Mitchell believed it had something to do with the unsupported cantilevered wing 'fluttering' at speed, making the aircraft dangerously unstable. His later seaplanes were lifted on lower-set wings judiciously supported with wire stays.

The Italians were back on form in 1926, winning at Norfolk, Virginia. This was the first event in which all teams fielded pilots from their armed forces. The military value of high-speed flight had by now been fully recognized. The RAF formed its High Speed Flight, an official band of top-flight pilots, mechanics and racing aircraft, at Felixstowe that year and, with their skill and dash, Supermarine trumped the Italians in Venice in 1927, when the RAF's Flight Lieutenant Webster won with Mitchell's latest 860-hp Napier-powered Supermarine S 5, at 281.28 mph. Britain took second and third places too.

The next race was in 1929. Now powered by Rolls-Royce's brand-new 37-litre, liquid-cooled 1,920-hp R-Type V12, a military engine with 'racing capabilities' developed without government funding, the latest Supermarine S 6, flown by Flying Officer Waghorn, completed the circuit over the Solent between Gosport and the Isle of Wight at 328.63 mph. One of the RAF team on the ground helping with preparations for the race was Aircraftsman Shaw, the former Colonel T. E. Lawrence, of Arabia fame. Lawrence went on to work at RAF Calshot, Hampshire, on the development of Scott-Paine's high-speed air-sea rescue boats.

Then, in 1931, Supermarine and the RAF won for a third time, thus ensuring permanent possession of the Schneider Trophy by Great Britain. Flight Lieutenant J. N. Boothman roared around the Solent circuit at 340.08 mph, the mighty R-Type under the nose of his S 6B seaplane pumping out a staggering 2,350 hp. A fortnight later, Boothman flew the victorious S 6B to a new world air speed record of 407.5 mph. The Schneider Trophy itself, a silver and bronze art nouveau confection in the guise of a winged figure embracing another floating decorously on the crest of a

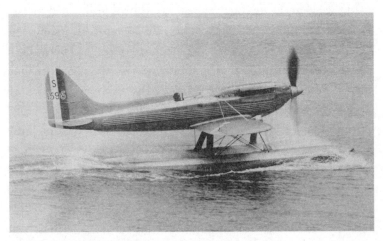

A Supermarine S 6B seaplane on the water at Calshot in 1931.

wave, is not quite as elegant as a Supermarine S 6B; if you must, you can see it on display in London's Science Museum.

Remarkably, the British government had been little help in the build-up to the 1931 event, despite its obvious importance to the flying fraternity, aircraft manufacturers and at least one of the coming generation of totalitarian dictators, Benito Mussolini. In a sky still filled with string and canvas biplanes, the streamlined Schneider aircraft must have seemed almost impossibly futuristic to an awed public – and to German aircraft designers such as the young Willy Messerschmitt, whose country's military development had been strictly limited by the 1919 Treaty of Versailles. Yet Ramsay MacDonald's Cabinet initially withdrew financial backing for the British entries in 1931, chiefly on grounds of cost, and refused permission for valuable RAF pilots to take part. They even had an expert witness: Sir Hugh Trenchard, Marshal of the Royal Air Force and very much a bomber man, said of the Schneider competition that he could see 'nothing of value in it'.

In the event, Dame Lucy Houston, a chorus girl turned society hostess, had flown to the rescue with a personal cheque for £100,000 written out to Supermarine. Dame Lucy had never been one to shy away from excitement. At sweet sixteen, and as the then Fanny Radmall, also known to various wealthy gentlemen as Poppy, she had eloped to Paris with the much older, and wealthy, married brewer Frederick Gretton. When Gretton died in 1882, he left his Lucy, or Fanny, or Poppy, £6,000 a year for life. Lucy's third marriage in 1924 to Sir Robert Paterson Houston, Bt, MP and shipping magnate, was a great success – at least in the sense that this decidedly unpopular man left her £5.5 million upon his sudden, and mysterious, death aboard his yacht *Liberty* just two years later. At the time of her donation, Dame Lucy, a former suffragette as well as showgirl, was a fanatical supporter of Mussolini. Far too many members of the British upper classes, and the media that supported them, were seduced by the causes of Fascism and anti-Semitism, but Dame Lucy gave her £100,000 to Supermarine partly as a grandiose snub to Ramsay MacDonald's Labour government and to socialism, both of which she despised.

Shamed by such private largesse, the government retaliated by announcing that RAF pilots could fly in the event after all. The Italians, meanwhile, backed by the munificence of Mussolini, were spending lavishly on the development and construction of the latest Macchi M 72 monoplane racer, its 24-cylinder, 50-litre Fiat engine rated at an astonishing 2,850 hp. Nevertheless, with Dame Lucy's help, the British won on the wings of Mitchell's charismatic and graceful S 6B. Curiously, although they had pushed the design of fast aircraft to impressive new limits and influenced the design of the very latest Supermarine contender, the Italians were to enter the Second World War with Macchi and Fiat monoplane fighters that were simply no match for their opponents. It was the Germans, still struggling to become a world power in the early 1930s and unable to take part in the Schneider contests, who went on quietly, behind the scenes, to develop the first truly effective high-speed warplanes.

The British government and Trenchard had been wrong to denigrate the Schneider air races. They did have an important impact on the development of a new generation of piston-engined fighter aircraft. They also led Mitchell and Supermarine into the world of purely military aircraft and thus, remarkably quickly, to the design of the Spitfire itself. Like anyone with any common sense in the aircraft industry, Mitchell had been well aware of the impact of the first generation of liquid-cooled, inline, V-configuration engines; they had proved their efficacy in the American victory in the 1923 Schneider event. Unlike conventional air-cooled rotary engines, inline engines were long and low: they allowed designers to shape streamlined noses which reduced the frontal area of their machines and, in turn, drag, and to obtain considerably higher speeds for a given power output.

Designed for outright speed, the Schneider machines themselves would have made poor fighter planes if they had been equipped with machine-guns and sent up into action. The pilots of the S 5 and S 6 racers had no forward view whatsoever from the cockpit and, even if they leaned out to either side, streamlined casings over the long cylinder heads blocked slipstream views. Only by banking the aircraft could the pilot see where he was going. The big, pedigree engines that drove these aircraft to such great speeds needed to be stripped and rebuilt frequently; they were not designed to cope with the rough and tumble of war. And yet in the design of these rip-roaring inline engines lay the outcome of the Battle of Britain and, to a significant degree, the destiny of the free world.

Richard Fairey was the first British aircraft manufacturer to pick up on the advantages of the Curtiss D-12 inline engine that helped the Americans take first and second places in the 1923 Schneider race, and to win again, very convincingly, in 1925. Work on the Curtiss V12 had begun at the end of the First World War. Initial development by Charles L. Kirkham, Glenn Curtiss's chief motor engineer, was taken up by his successor, the appropriately named Arthur Nutt. Working with the acoustics engineer, Dr S. A. Reed, who had developed a new type of one-piece aluminium airscrew, or propeller, Nutt came up with the fully fledged D-12 aero-engine in 1921. It was to prove a world-beater.

Fairey paid a visit to the Curtiss factory in upstate New York and brought back, in the privacy of his ocean-liner stateroom, a complete D-12 and its advanced high-speed Reed propeller. Back in Britain, Fairey fitted the V12 unit to a modified biplane he called the Fox. It was a bomber, and yet it proved to be very quick indeed. In fact, it was at least 50 mph faster than any other British military plane, including the latest biplane fighters. Fairey campaigned for the bulk purchase of D-12s, but the government, aware of their performance yet peeved by the fact that they were foreign, turned to the British engine-builders Napier and Rolls-Royce to meet the challenge. Napier declined, but a Curtiss D-12 was packed off to Rolls-Royce in Derby, where it was taken to pieces under the beady eye of Henry Royce himself and analysed. This led directly to Royce's 22-litre Kestrel V12 and the gruff and extremely powerful R-Type V12 of 1929. Both were designed by Rolls-Royce's Arthur J. Rowledge, and the R-Type was not only to take Mitchell's S 6B seaplane to victory, and the world speed record, in 1931, but also to send later marks of Spitfires into high-flying, high-speed combat from 1942 onwards. For this engine was to become the burly 37-litre Rolls-Royce Griffon, designed by Arthur Rubbra. But long before it was installed in these beefier Spitfires, an ex-Schneider racing R-Type engine powered Malcolm Campbell and his Bluebird through the 300-mph barrier on land (301.129 mph, to be precise) at Bonneville Salt Flats, Utah, in 1933, while a brace of these bellowing V12s, pumping out 4,700 hp, took George Eyston and his Thunderbolt car to 357.5 mph across the same terrain in 1938. This was every bit as fast as a Mk I Spitfire.

Development of the R-Type led, in turn, to the design of a smaller, 27-litre Rolls-Royce V12, designed for sustained high-speed flight. This was the work of Rolls-Royce engineer

R. W. Harvey-Bailey, assisted by James Ellor, who had been involved with the design and development of the R-Type. It was to be named Merlin. Now, thanks to Schneider, Curtiss, Dame Lucy Houston and other odd and unexpected characters gathering in the wings of the Supermarine stage, the threads of the Spitfire were being drawn together. However, it would still take a leap of engineering imagination before Mitchell started work on his greatest achievement, by which time Adolf Hitler had announced plans, in violation of the Treaty of Versailles, to expand the strength of the Wehrmacht, the German army, through conscription, to 500,000 troops. Indeed, just two days after the prototype Spitfire made its maiden flight on 5 March 1936, Hitler sent his troops to reoccupy the now demilitarized Rhineland.

In 1930, at the height of the Schneider air races, the Air Ministry issued its specification number F.7/30 for a new RAF fighter armed with four .303 machine-guns. Mitchell responded, during 1932 and 1933, with a strangely ungainly monoplane with an open cockpit, fixed undercarriage sheathed in the aero-industry's equivalent of plus-fours or pantaloons, an inverted gull wing, and a top speed, courtesy of a steam-cooled 660-hp Rolls-Royce Goshawk engine, of just 228 mph. Both the wing shape and the awkward undercarriage were necessary to cope with the complex demands of the Goshawk; this engine's coolant evaporated at a rapid rate and had to be condensed back into liquid, from steam, before it could be channelled to cooling sleeves around the cylinders. The steam had to expand somewhere inside the airframe if it was to be returned, after cooling, as water back to the engine; this was done in a rather awkward flow between the leading edges of the wings, especially enlarged for the purpose, and the thick trousers, or sleeves, around the wheels.

It was a cumbersome system. Not only did it lead to a clumsy-looking aircraft, but this overwrought plumbing also proved to be inefficient. Test pilots, warned to look out for a red light on the instrument panel indicating an overheating engine, recalled that the light went on at take-off or thereabouts and glowed red for the entire flight. But if the choice of the Goshawk as powerplant had been an odd one, then the decision to go for flapless wings was positively bizarre. Flaps allow an aircraft to fly slowly without stalling; this enables pilots to approach airfields at safe speeds. An aircraft without flaps must necessarily come in to land at high speed. You can get a feel of this at home by making dart-like paper aircraft from stiff paper, first with and then without flaps. The difference in the way they fly will be marked. Flapless landings would have been particularly dangerous in the dark too, at a time when the Air Ministry was looking for an all-weather fighter.

First flown in February 1934, the Type 224 performed poorly in comparison with its several rivals. In the event, the Air Ministry plumped for the 257-mph Gloster Gladiator biplane powered by an elegantly straightforward 830-hp Bristol Mercury radial engine. The last RAF biplane, in service from 1935, the Gladiator flew beautifully and during the Second World War was to fight over Norway, Greece, the Middle East and the North African desert and, most famously, in the defence of Malta. It must have felt familiar to pilots of the RAF's existing frontline 1930s fighter, the Hawker Fury. This pretty machine, designed by Sydney Camm, dated from 1927 and was to remain in frontline service with the RAF until immediately before the outbreak of the Second World War. It went on to fly with the South African Air Force against the Italians in East Africa and, heroically, with the Yugoslav Air Force against the Luftwaffe in the spring of 1941. The Fury was a joy to fly. It was a piece of cake to take off and land; it was as nimble as proverbial Jack, who flew over the candlestick, and because it was so immediately responsive to any change in the power setting of its Rolls-Royce V12 Kestrel engine, it was ideal for formation flying. This was the 200-mph machine with which the RAF wowed the crowds at the famous Hendon air shows of the 1930s, an aircraft that did much to make the RAF sparkle in the public's imagination. The Supermarine 224 was lacklustre in comparison, nor was it a great deal faster.

It was as if the Type 224 had been a mirror of Mitchell's own less than happy condition. In May 1933 he had been diagnosed with bowel cancer. That August, he very nearly died on the operating table. And yet, well before the Air Ministry rejected the Type 224 in 1935, Mitchell, now patched up with a colostomy bag and often in pain, was more than busy at work on the Supermarine Type 300. Here was the giant leap of the imagination needed to supersede the RAF's Furies and Gladiators and, more importantly, to convince both the Air Ministry and the RAF that a modern, multi-gunned, high-speed monoplane fighter was an essential tool in a future war in which aircraft would play a leading role.

Many senior air officials, and notably Lord Trenchard, still preached a doctrine of air power resolutely in favour of strategic bombing. (The RAF had, in fact, been busy refining such techniques in Iraq, where it had been terror-bombing the civilian population ever since that unhappy country's creation in 1921.) Hugh Trenchard had been Chief of Air Staff during the First World War, and the founding father of the RAF in 1918. A veteran, before then, of the Boer War, which ended the year before powered flight began and in which he had served with the Royal Scots Fusiliers, he was known as 'Boom' Trenchard, because of his commanding voice, which tended to rise above everyone else's. He was thirty-nine when he learned to fly, at Thomas Sopwith's flying school at Brooklands, Surrey, and in many respects his thinking had evolved little since the 1914-18 war. He was appointed Chief of Air Staff under Winston Churchill in 1919, and stayed put until his retirement in 1929. He even went so far as to tell Churchill that, after his successes in quelling disturbances among uppity natives in Iraq and Somaliland, where his machines also dropped poison gas bombs, the RAF could be used to stamp out 'industrial disturbances or risings' at home in Britain.

Trenchard's strategic bombing doctrine was still enshrined in Air Ministry dogma as late as 1936, by which time the prototype Spitfire was proving its prowess, and notoriously so in Sir John Slessor's book, *Airpower and Armies*. Slessor was Chief of Plans in the Air Ministry and a prominent member of the defence establishment. He admitted, after the war, that the Air Ministry's all but blind belief in the capability of the long-range strategic bomber had been 'a matter of faith'. It certainly was. In 1937, the RAF conducted a test of its latest bombing techniques. Thirty obsolete aircraft were scattered in a 1,000-yard circle. During the course of a week, Bomber Command attacked the target from high and low level. It managed to destroy two aircraft, damage eleven beyond repair, put six temporarily out of action, and missed the other eleven altogether. And yet, right up until the Battle of Britain, the majority at the Air Ministry continued to argue that fighter and air defence were a waste of time and money because the bomber would always get through, and that the only way to defeat the enemy was to clobber him hard by using British bombers to attack his home bases. Their confidence was misplaced. The RAF's own light bomber, the twin-engined Bristol

Blenheim, had first flown in military guise in 1936. It seemed to be very fast indeed, further proof that the bomber could hold its own with fighters. But when war came, Blenheim squadrons suffered heavy losses: despite its top speed of 266 mph, the Mk IV version of the bomber was over 80 mph slower than the Messerschmitt Bf 109E-3.

In the event, it was Neville Chamberlain, the British Prime Minister long accused of appeasing Hitler and Mussolini, who listened to a very different voice, that of Air Chief Marshal Sir Hugh Dowding. A former First World War fighter pilot, Dowding had gone solo in just one hour and forty minutes. A precise, determined and quietly brilliant man, he was to ensure that suitable fighter aircraft and well-trained pilots and ground staff were available in just sufficient numbers in the summer of 1940 to prevent Hitler from launching his Operation Sealion, the invasion of Britain.

The son of a schoolmaster, Dowding was born in Moffat, Scotland, in 1882. Educated at Winchester and the Royal Military Academy in Woolwich, he served with the Royal Artillery Garrison in Gibraltar, Ceylon and Hong Kong before spending six years in India with mountain artillery troops. On his return to England, he learned to fly and joined the Royal Flying Corps. As a flight commander in France at the time of the Battle of the Somme, he clashed with Trenchard, who insisted pilots remained in the frontline for as long as possible without a period of rest and recuperation. Dowding disagreed. He was promoted, however, sent back to England and kept out of Trenchard's hair. Four years after Trenchard's retirement, Dowding was promoted to Air Marshal, knighted and appointed a member of the Air Council for Supply and Research. Now the fighter aircraft, and its pilots, had their champion in place. While Trenchard's successors continued to bang on about bombing, Dowding paved the way for the Spitfire, the Hurricane and radar, an invention that was to make these fighters especially effective during the Battle of Britain.

Even then, as late as June 1938, an Air Staff memorandum declared: 'The speed of modern bombers is so great that it is only worthwhile to attack them under conditions which allow no relative motion between the fighter and its target. The fixed-gun fighter with guns firing ahead can only realize these conditions by attacking the bomber from dead astern.' In the event, on 3 September 1939, the day Britain declared war on Germany, the RAF had a bomber force all but incapable of carrying out daylight operations in the face of opposition from the Luftwaffe, and effectively unable to hit targets by night. If it had not been for a few enlightened but stubborn men such as 'Stuffy' Dowding and Chamberlain, there would have been no convincing air defence either, and the Battle of Britain would have been lost in a matter of days. Dowding positively encouraged Chamberlain's policy of appeasement; while the Prime Minister flew to Munich believing sincerely that he would secure 'peace in our time', Dowding was playing for time. He wanted Spitfires, and Hurricanes too, and plenty of them, together with pilots who would know how to make the best of them when Hitler finally lashed out at Britain.

The Germans had been far more realistic about what they could expect from air power. The experience the Luftwaffe's Condor Legion had gained during the Spanish Civil War suggested that terror bombing was not just a waste of time, but counter-productive. The air attack on Guernica, for example, had turned the Basques not just against Germany but, to a significant degree, towards communism. The Germans instead built up a tactical air force that would work hand-in-hand with Blitzkrieg forces on the ground. (The arrangement was to prove highly successful in both Poland in September 1939 and France in May 1940. Indeed, it was only when Hitler ordered the Luftwaffe to concentrate its efforts on the bombing of London in the summer of 1940, rather than press home its successful attacks on struggling RAF fighter bases and aircraft factories, that he ensured he lost the Battle of Britain.) The brass hats at the Air Ministry, meanwhile, remained largely unaware of just how significant increases in speed and advances in technology had been between the delivery of the RAF's beloved Hawker Furies and the arrival of the Spitfire.

To get a better idea of the pilot's point of view, Mitchell had taken up flying lessons in December 1933, winning his wings in July 1934. Furthermore, although with less than three years to live, he worked apace not just on the design and development of the Spitfire, but also on that of a four-engined long-range bomber, which would have been able to carry the same bomb-load as a Lancaster at Spitfire speed, a fast flying boat and a four-cannon, heavy-duty fighter. The bomber and fast flying boat projects never came to fruition, although the fuselages of two bombers were under construction by the time the Supermarine factory was heavily bombed in 1940. These fascinating sections of an aircraft that would almost certainly have saved the lives of many Bomber Command aircrews, were destroyed, together with the plans for their design and construction. The first four-cannon fighter duly emerged from another manufacturer in the form of the twin-engined Westland Whirlwind, but this was to be quickly out-classed by the Spitfire, which from 1942 onwards was equipped with both a cannon armament and the mighty Griffon engine.

Towards the end of 1934, meanwhile, Rolls-Royce had unveiled its 790-hp PV12 (private venture, 12-cylinder) engine. Work had begun on the 27-litre supercharged V12 in 1932, with the Air Ministry agreeing to finance its development the following year. By 1935, the Merlin was producing 990 hp, as near as dammit to the 1,000 hp promised by Sir Henry Royce, who had initiated the project a year before he died. Both Sydney Camm at Hawker and Mitchell at Supermarine knew this was the engine for their new fighters.

In November 1935, Vickers gave Supermarine the necessary funding to design a PV12-powered monoplane fighter. Merlin and Spitfire had come together. Within a month, progressive elements in the otherwise conservative Air Ministry spotted a potential winner in the making. The myth endures that the Spitfire, like the Merlin, was a privately funded project until late in the day. This is untrue. Dowding and others were right behind it. The Air Ministry issued a contract for the new fighter, officially designated F.37/34, in December 1934, and handed over £10,000 for construction of the prototype.

The seductive streamlined shape of the monocoque aluminium fighter, with its thin wings, stressed aluminium skin construction and faired cockpit with Perspex canopy, emerged quickly, although at first in the guise of a wooden mock-up shown to Air Ministry officials in April 1935. The elliptical wings, largely the work of Beverley Shenstone, who had worked with Ernst Heinkel in Germany, were a direct result of Mitchell's demand for a thin wing, but one thick enough – and structurally strong enough – as it met the fuselage to contain both wheels and weapons. The number of guns increased to eight .303 Brownings, following a recommendation by Squadron Leader Ralph Sorely of the

Operational Requirements section at the Air Ministry, so the wing had to be long enough to find space for them. 'The ellipse,' said Shenstone, 'was simply the shape that allowed us the thinnest possible wing with sufficient room inside it to carry the necessary structure and the things we wanted to cram in.'

Shenstone was always keen to insist in later years that the Spitfire's famous wing shape was not informed by that of the elegant Heinkel He 70, a light mail plane and potential Luftwaffe dive-bomber that first flew in 1932. As it was, Rolls-Royce was so enthusiastic about the potential of the He 70 as a flying test-bed for prototype engines that it sent a team to Germany to buy one of the aircraft direct from Heinkel. The German government approved the deal, but only in return for a number of Rolls-Royce Kestrel engines. (Intriguingly, the first prototype Messerschmitt Bf 109 was to fly with one of these British V12 engines under its bonnet.) Mitchell, too, was well aware of the He 70, whose design would lead, in a different direction, to that of the Heinkel He 111 twin-engined bomber, an aircraft that Spitfires would be sent up to chase from British skies.

Meetings and the sharing of technical information between British and German manufacturers were par for the course throughout the 1930s. Supermarine employees were quite used to the sight of German flying boats, including the Dornier Do 26 Wal, together with Blohm und Voss Ha 139 floatplanes, decked out in full Nazi regalia, berthed alongside the Woolston works. Although these were classified as 'mail planes', Supermarine staff knew them as 'spy planes'. Did visiting German engineers and pilots then spot what appeared to be the fuselage of such top-secret designs as a prototype twin-engined Spitfire in the rafters of the works? Did they really learn anything that would have made them design their own aircraft any differently? It appears not. Although well aware of technical developments on either side of the growing political gulf between Great Britain and Germany, aero-engineers in both countries followed their noses. Global design was some way off.

For pilots, the shape of the Spitfire's wing, whatever its true design lineage, was a godsend. Because the angle the Spitfire wing presents to the airflow is greater nearer the fuselage, where the wing is much thicker, than it is towards the thin wing tips, the pilot would feel an impending stall as a slight wobble well before the wings themselves stalled. This was particularly important in combat as, in a tight turn and on full throttle, the aircraft needed to be kept just on the edge of stalling to achieve the minimum turning circle. This made the Spitfire an extremely safe and forgiving aircraft to fly, allowing pilots to make extremely tight turns and so outmanoeuvre their opponents.

Squadron Leader Sorely visited the Supermarine works in April 1935 to discuss the gun requirements with Mitchell and his team. He explained how in combat against the latest high-speed, all-metal German bombers, a fighter pilot would only be able to get in two-second bursts against his target. He had calculated that to cause significant damage, or to destroy the enemy aircraft, the Spitfire would need eight of the latest Brownings firing at the rate of eighteen rounds a second. This would pump 288 rounds into a bomber in a two-second burst. With 300 rounds per gun, the Spitfire would have sufficient ammunition for eight such bursts. The guns fitted, just, and then only if they were stretched out at ever wider intervals across the wings and fed by long, low ammunition boxes. If the Spitfire's slim wings meant that eight machine-guns were a tight fit, then there was no possibility of them being used to carry fuel. So petrol for the Merlin, at first

87- and later 100-octane, was stored in a small tank mounted between the engine and the cockpit. As a result, the aircraft had a short range and was always best used as an interceptor.

A new and highly efficient type of radiator developed by Fred Meredith at the Royal Aircraft Establishment and Rolls-Royce's adoption of ethylene glycol as a coolant allowed Mitchell to design a very slim nose for the new fighter. The neat little Meredith radiator was mounted under the starboard wing. The header tank for the coolant, though, was situated at the very front of the aircraft and was vulnerable to enemy fire. Although a highly effective coolant, ethylene glycol, invented by the French chemist Charles Wurtz in 1859 but not put into mass industrial production until 1937, is flammable.

At first, the Merlin was designed, like the Goshawk that powered the Type 224, to be steam-cooled, and this is why the Spitfire's wings have pronounced leading edges; these would have been used to help cool the steam. Although such a strong leading edge was unnecessary once Rolls-Royce adapted the Merlin for ethylene glycol cooling, the shape was retained. By happy accident, it contributed to what proved to be a superb aerodynamic configuration. This, though, is very much the story of the development of the Spitfire. The design process was rapid. It needed to change quickly in response to new demands, specifications and inventions. It was, in the very best sense, a resolution of numerous compromises, and a marriage of the best available aircraft technology at the time. Mitchell's genius was to fuse these concerns, practicalities and availabilities together into one beautiful and highly effective machine. If the Spitfire was a work of art, then it was not intended as such, even if it was produced by men with a naturally fine sense of economy, efficiency and line.

As recently as the autumn of 2005, there was a wonderful correspondence in the letters pages of the *Daily Telegraph* about the origins of the Spitfire design. Tim Cope from Wokingham, Berkshire, made the point, pithily, that 'The Hurricane was an all-British design by Sydney Camm. The basic shape of the Spitfire was copied from the German Heinkel 70 . . .' The inference is that the Spitfire was not all British. This, though, would not have been a concern of Mitchell's. He wanted only to create the finest piston-engined fighter of his day. One can argue that the He 70 played its part in Shenstone's wing, and that Mitchell's aerodynamicist was a Canadian. One could further argue that the Merlin engine was a development of the American Curtiss D-12, and, of course, that Mitchell had been influenced by Italian design during the Schneider years, so that the Italians too had therefore played some small part in the development of the Spitfire. Yet Mitchell's design, like so much great engineering, or art, was ultimately his own brilliant synthesis of ideas drawn from across the aero-industry. It was designed and built in Southampton. It has long been a symbol of a free Britain, and indeed of a British spirit that, always hard to define, can be felt in the heart whenever a Spitfire is seen or heard, on screen or in the air.

The unpainted Spitfire prototype, K5054, all external rivets cut smooth and polished, was finally wheeled out of the shed at Woolston alongside the River Itchen in February 1936. The flush-rivet construction had been immensely time-consuming, yet gave the aircraft a slippery profile as it cut through the air. Glorious experiments, seemingly Heath Robinson-like yet entirely practical, were conducted on K5054 in later months, using split peas in place of dome-headed rivets, and these allowed the Supermarine engineers to strike a balance between the number of expensive flush and cheaper domed rivets used in the making of each Spitfire. One extra split pea here or there could increase drag and thus lower the aircraft's performance. In the event, the Spitfire development team settled on a happy, more or less fifty-fifty compromise. By 29 February 1936, the Spitfire had cost Supermarine £14,637, about £600,000 today. Add in Rolls-Royce's bill, and the all-in cost of K5054 appears to have been £20,765. Given that the government had shelled out £12,478, and Rolls-Royce £7,500, the total cost to Supermarine itself was £787. The Spitfire had been, to say the very least, a bargain.

The Merlin engine of the smooth-skinned K5054 was spirited into life above the cry of gulls and hoots of boats that crisp February morning while Mitchell's team conducted the necessary tests. K5054 was then dismantled and taken by road to the Supermarine hangar at Eastleigh airfield, better known today as Southampton airport. This stood very near to Southern Railway's principal locomotive works, where, from 1946, Oliver Bulleid's 'Battle of Britain'-class Pacifics were built. One of these fine, modern steam locomotives, shrouded in what its designer described as 'air-smoothed casing', was named 'Spitfire'. Another, 'Winston Churchill', steamed the great man's coffin from Waterloo to its final resting place at Bladon, Oxfordshire, in 1965. The last trip made in normal, revenue-earning service by a 'Battle of Britain' Pacific was a perishable goods train running from Weymouth to Westbury on 9 July 1967 with wagonloads of tomatoes from the Channel Islands. The locomotive was 34052, 'Lord Dowding'. Britain never learned to treat this great warrior well.

On the afternoon of 5 March 1936, Vickers's chief test pilot, Captain Joseph 'Mutt' Summers, arrived. He had been flown to

Eastleigh in a Miles Hawk, piloted by his colleague Jeffrey Quill, from the RAF's test establishment at Martlesham Heath, Suffolk, where he had been showing RAF top brass over a very different aircraft, the idiosyncratic single-engined Vickers Wellesley bomber. At 4.35 p.m., Summers signalled 'Chocks away' and Mitchell's pugnacious little aircraft – some thirty feet long, just over eight feet high and with a wingspan of thirty-seven feet – vaulted into a clear sky. Eight minutes later, Summers and K5054 were back on the ground. 'I don't want anything touched,' he said, meaning not that the Spitfire was perfect, but that he wanted to try it again with the controls exactly as he had left them. With a new propeller in place, Summers flew the aircraft for twenty-three minutes the following day. After the fourth flight, and a new engine, Summers left the test-flying to his assistants, Jeffrey Quill and George Pickering.

The Spitfire, as they soon discovered, was good – very good indeed, but not perfect. The rudder was oversensitive, and the top speed was a disappointing 330 mph, no faster than Sydney Camm's new Merlin-powered Hawker Hurricane, which had flown five months earlier. There was also a hint that at 380 mph, which the Spitfire would easily reach in a dive, it was likely to develop wing flutter, the very same condition that had done for Mitchell's S 4 racer during the Schneider years.

Hectic work on the aircraft saw her back in the air on 11 May, resplendent in a coat of pale blue paint. She looked every inch the epitome of a new generation of fighter planes. Quill flew K5054 as Mitchell watched its progress from the passenger seat of a Miles Falcon flying alongside, with John Yoxall taking the first air-to-air photographs of the newly tuned machine. A new and better-shaped wooden propeller saw the Spitfire reach 348 mph in level flight in mid-May. Towards the end of the month, Summers flew K5054 to Martlesham Heath, where Flight Lieutenant Humphrey Edwardes-Jones did the honours for the RAF. He had been given orders to fly the aircraft and then to make his report as soon as he landed, by telephone, to the Air Ministry. The men at the Ministry were very interested in the Spitfire now. They badly needed a winner, especially since the Luftwaffe's fast and light Messerschmitt Bf 109 was up and flying over Spain, and with lethal purpose.

After nearly pranging the Spitfire – he almost forgot to let the wheels down – Edwardes-Jones promptly called Air Vice Marshal Wilfrid Freeman at the Air Ministry. Was the Spitfire any good? Yes, replied Edwardes-Jones, as long as it was equipped with an indicator that would confirm that the undercarriage was either up or down. Clever chap. With this one phone call, the Spitfire's

The Spitfire prototype, K5054, being readied for a test flight in 1936.

place in history was assured. Just over a week later, Supermarine received an order for 310 Spitfires. It was impossible for the company to cope with such a large order, so plans were made to outsource much of the work.

Meanwhile, K5054 was displayed in front of a thrilled public at the RAF Pageant at Hendon at the end of June. King Edward VIII came to clamber over the new fighter at Martlesham Heath in early July, while on the eleventh of the month, Edwardes-Jones gave himself another fright. He took K5054 up to 34,700 feet, higher than he had ever flown before, and watched as vapour trails streamed back from the exhaust pipes along the aircraft's nose. He had never seen these before. The Spitfire was taking RAF pilots into entirely new territory.

Throughout 1937 and 1938, K5054, now painted in contemporary RAF camouflage – earth brown and dark green on top, silver below – was subject to test after test. When the aircraft was fitted with guns, it was discovered they would not fire at altitude. They were freezing up. So a way had to be devised for the armament to be warmed by the engine. It was a fiddly business and took time to get right. New exhaust pipes added 70 hp to the Merlin engine and increased top speed to 360 mph. Wing flutter was still a potential problem and K5054, for all her knife-edge manoeuvrability, was limited to an absolute maximum speed of 380 mph. Her pilots, however, learned to pull gs – uncomfortable multiples of the force of gravity at work on both aircraft and pilot – that would cause them to black out, momentarily, in sensationally fast, tight turns.

In July 1938, the first production Spitfire, K9787, emerged from Supermarine's Woolston works. It was time for K5054 to take a back seat. It would be wonderful to be able to see this truly historic aircraft preserved, and even flying today, but sadly she came to grief at Farnborough on 4 September 1939, the day after Neville Chamberlain announced over the wireless that Great Britain was at war with Germany. Flight Lieutenant 'Spinner' White had landed badly and died soon afterwards. K5054 was a write-off.

By this time Mitchell was dead, killed by the cancer that had returned during 1936. He was admitted to hospital in London in February 1937, but his doctors said there was nothing they could do for him. He was forced to stop work, though he still liked nothing better – aside from watching his garden grow and seeing the songbirds that flitted in and out of it – than sitting in his beloved black and yellow 1932 Rolls-Royce and watching K5054 take to the air. In April 1937 he flew to Austria, on board a De Havilland Rapide, to spend time in the clinic of a cancer specialist in Vienna. Again, there was nothing to be done. Back in Southampton, Mitchell, uncomplaining to the last, put his estate in order. He died on 11 June at the age of forty-two.

Joseph Smith, his chief draughtsman, was appointed to replace Mitchell. Another quiet and modest man, 'Joe' Smith took up seamlessly where 'RJ' had left off. He was a consummate development engineer and kept working on the aircraft until 1947, when the last Spitfire was built. The production Spitfire was essentially Smith's work. An entirely new set of drawings was produced in a busy office with more than a hundred engineers and draughtsmen. The aircraft that Jeffrey Quill first put through its paces on 15 May 1938 was different in several fundamental ways from Mitchell's prototype. Most importantly, the internal structure of the wing was beefed up. Now the Spitfire could be dived at up to 470 mph. Flaps were given greater scope. The fuel tankage was increased from seventy-five to eighty-four imperial gallons. An RAF-approved flying panel was installed. A new starter motor helped get the Merlin, now rated at 1,030 hp, whirring. A new 'blister' canopy offered extra headroom for pilots above jockey height. An engine-driven hydraulic undercarriage was installed. And the twin-bladed, fixed-pitch wooden propellers fitted to the first seventy-seven production aircraft were replaced by a De Havilland three-bladed, two-pitch design. This increased the top speed of the Spitfire very marginally, and lifted its ceiling another 3,000 feet, yet reduced its rate of climb from 2,530 to 2,175 feet per minute; the problem was finally solved in March 1940 when the new Rotol constant-speed, three-bladed propeller enabled a best climb of 2,905 feet per minute. The new props were fitted to all Mk IIs, while Mk Is were updated with constant speed airscrews just in time for the Battle of Britain.

A standard Mk I, K9834, was modified for an attempt at the world speed record. The 'Speed Spitfire', its Merlin producing a sensational 2,160 hp, first took to the air on 11 November 1938, although there appears to be no record of how fast this machine actually flew. Willy Messerschmitt, however, was ahead of the speed game. His sensational Me 209 V1, first flown on 1 August 1938, was clearly a force to be reckoned with. On 26 April 1939, with Flugkapitän Fritz Wendel at the controls, it set a new world record – 469.22 mph over a specified course in level flight – that was not to be broken by a piston-engined aircraft for over thirty years. (In August 1969, the American pilot Darryl G. Greenmyer took a highly modified 3,100-hp Grumman F8F-2 Bearcat fighter up to 483.041 mph; this was raised to just over 522 mph by another Bearcat in 1989.) In 1938, Supermarine knew they were unlikely to beat the Me 209 V1, even though few were convinced by German propaganda broadcasts claiming that the Me 209 was a new type of frontline fighter. The effort invested in K9834 had not been wasted, however, as it became the basis for the run of very successful high-flying and high-speed Spitfires used for photo-reconnaissance duties throughout the Second World War.

Was the attempt on the world record a hangover from the days of the Schneider Trophy? Or was it intended as a kind of marketing promotion for the new Spitfire? Supermarine had produced a smart sales brochure at much the same time as K9384 made her maiden flight. Among countries expressing an interest in buying were Greece, Turkey and Estonia. But production of the Spitfire took off slowly and, as it turned out, the RAF needed every machine it could get.

With modifications made by the end of 1938, the Spitfire was very nearly ready for battle. By September 1939, 187 Spitfires served ten RAF squadrons. Luckily, there was time during the Phoney War to make further improvements. The three-bladed constant-speed metal propeller, 100-octane petrol imported from the United States, armour plating behind and beneath the pilot's seat, protective sheeting for the fuel tank and a toughened glass windscreen, all added to the fighting strength, and weight, of the aircraft. Although it saw some limited action during the Battle of France, principally over the evacuation beaches at Dunkirk, the Spitfire was largely held back at home on the controversial orders of Air Chief Marshal Dowding. He had no intention of allowing Britain to be unprotected when the Luftwaffe struck. By July 1940, with the Battle of Britain about to begin, Dowding had equipped nineteen squadrons with Spitfires.

A month earlier, production of the Spitfire Mk II, with an initial order for 1,000 aircraft, had begun at a vast new factory at Castle

Bromwich in the West Midlands. This had been set up under the direction of Lord Nuffield, the car magnate. Despite Nuffield's depth of experience in the motor industry, the sheer complexity of the Spitfire proved to be too much of a challenge. It was never an easy aircraft to make. Lord Beaverbrook, Churchill's minister for aircraft production, turned the Castle Bromwich plant over to Vickers. Management was completely reorganized, while Joe Smith's engineering team made its way up from Southampton to show how the job could be done. The sheer scale of the Castle Bromwich plant represented official, and perhaps national, faith in the Spitfire. Now Mitchell's fighter was in full production, as it would be throughout the war. It was time for the Spitfire, and all its artistry, wizardry and complexity, to do battle.

CHAPTER II

THE THIN BLUE LINE

B ENTLEY Priory has about it a dreamlike quality, even though the guards on duty at the gate, wearing battle fatigues and toting the latest rapid-fire rifles, remind you that this intriguing country house, enlarged and remodelled by Sir John Soane from 1788 for John Hamilton, the First Marquess of Abercorn, and set in London's fast-disappearing green belt, is still a working RAF base.

In July 1936, Air Chief Marshal Hugh Sir Dowding walked here from 'Montrose', his Stanmore home, and showed his security pass to the sergeant on duty at the guardhouse. He had just been appointed head of the newly formed RAF Fighter Command. 'Stuffy', as he was known throughout the force, chose the south-facing library as his office. It looks out, then as now, over a sculpted Italianate garden and on, across a big sky, towards Harrow-on-the-Hill, marked by the tall spire of St Mary's church. The north London suburbs, which were spreading their red-brick and pebble-dash tentacles between here and Harrow even as Dowding was making plans for the defence of the realm, are completely invisible from the tall library windows. It remains a romantic view, one that conjures up a kind of idealized England whose freedoms, traditions and eccentricities were worth fighting for in 1939 and,

Air Chief Marshal Sir Hugh Dowding (right) escorts King George VI and Queen Elizabeth on a visit to Bentley Priory in September 1940.

of course, very much still are. Standing on the terrace outside the library under an icy, crisp blue sky, I can hear, in my mind's ear, the rumble and whistling roar of a Merlin engine, set to some stirring anthem composed, perhaps, by William Walton.

The Priory, originally founded as a religious community in the twelfth century, and later flogged off by Henry VIII, was bought by the fledgling RAF, for £25,000, in 1926. From 1908 to 1922 it had been what I imagine to have been a St Trinian's-style girls' school. Before that it was a hotel, run from 1882 by a Mr Frederick Gordon, who had paid out of his own pocket for the extension of the railway to Stanmore in the vain hope of drumming up guests. Even then, it was a hike uphill from the station and the hotel was not a success. Its previous owner, Sir John Kelk, the civil engineering contractor who had built Alexandra Palace in north London, had spent lavishly on additions to the house, including an imposing Italianate bell tower, but he was resident for less than two decades. Before Kelk, the Dowager Queen Adelaide, wife of William IV and mother of Queen Victoria, who herself visited the house many times in the late 1840s, spent her sunset years here. Today, glass-fibre replicas of a Battle of Britain Spitfire and Hurricane point, at threatening angles of attack, at what were once her bedroom windows. Pitt the Younger and the Duke of Wellington, the hero of Waterloo, were frequent guests of the Hamiltons at Bentley Priory during the Napoleonic Wars, the last time Britain had been threatened with invasion, as was Lord Nelson, the hero of Trafalgar and lover of the attitude-striking Lady Hamilton, who was, one imagines from those gorgeous, pouting portraits of her by George Romney, a bit of a spitfire herself.

So here was a house, quintessentially English, that was, in its peculiar and particular ways, a perfect base for Wellington's and Nelson's successor. With Dowding in charge, a slight makeover to its fabric was necessary. Nothing too drastic, of course, although the centre of the south drawing-room floor was cut away so that an Operations Room could be installed below, with a gallery above, around which Dowding and his commanders could prowl as they directed the show. Although the Ops Room was later moved to a deep concrete bunker in the grounds during the Blitz, and the drawing-room floor restored, the Luftwaffe, while hitting the new inner Metroland suburbs, failed to bomb Bentley Priory, as if its pilots knew such an outrage would be in very poor taste.

The house is a temple of sorts for the RAF; it is the service's memorial and shrine. Its lofty rooms brim with paintings, sculptures, tapestries, stained-glass windows and other artworks celebrating the RAF's greatest achievements over the best part of ninety years. Busts of Hermann Goering, Commander-in-Chief of the Luftwaffe and thus Dowding's rival, and his leader, Adolf Hitler, flown back from Germany at the end of the Second World War, skulk under Soane's magnificent central cantilevered Portland stone stair. 'High Flight' is inscribed above the door to the bar. The holy of holies at Bentley Priory is, of course, Dowding's office. When you enter, it seems as if the great man has just stepped out for a moment. Despite a fire in 1979, things are very much as they were. Here are the Bakelite telephones the Air Chief Marshal used to call Downing Street and his squadron commanders. Here, in a cabinet, is his pilot's licence. There, framed on the wall, is the famously terse memorandum he sent to the Air Ministry in April 1940, explaining why he would not allow any more of his pilots or his fighters to be sent to bases in France: he wanted his squadrons ready, and in tip-top condition, to react when the fight came to these shores.

Dowding, as the decor and contents of his office suggest, was the very opposite of Hermann Goering. The Reichsmarshal cut a flamboyant and larger-than-life figure; fuelled by a prodigious intake of drink and drugs, he liked nothing so much as shooting game or playing the society host. Goering had also been a First World War fighter pilot: he took over command of Manfred von Richthofen's Geschwader I, or Flying Circus, after the Red Baron's death in the air, and his mounts, Fokker D VIIs, were painted either an outrageous mauve and yellow or virginal white. His personal score of enemy aircraft shot down by 11 November 1918 was twenty-two. Dowding, meanwhile, was quietly spoken, upright, teetotal, correct, devoutly Christian, a widower and withdrawn. He was horrified at the thought of civilian casualties in time of war, and taken aback by Stanley Baldwin's view that 'the only defence is offence, which means that you have to kill more women and children more quickly than the enemy if you want to save yourself'.

It is easy to imagine Hugh Trenchard, no fan of Dowding, licking his lips at the former Tory Prime Minister's sentiment. For Dowding, however, 'the best defence of the country is fear of the fighter'. He was to be proved right. His spirit, I think, much resembles that of the English army and its Welsh archers under the inspired leadership of Henry V as it faced what appeared to be the crushing might of the French cavalry at Agincourt in 1415. The French, in all their armoured finery, preening and pouting, were confident that they were the masters of the moment. The English, hungry and racked by dysentery, were dug in behind a wall of pointed staves, as if creating an island shore between themselves and the enemy. When the heavily armoured horsemen charged, Henry's archers let loose with the fifteenth-century equivalent of Browning machine-guns – arrows from their powerful longbows. These archers were the Spitfire pilots of their day, and Henry's aggressively defensive tactics paid off. Now, in 1940, it was Dowding's turn to face the might of the Luftwaffe, which, seen largely through the distorting mirror of Nazi propaganda, appeared invincible.

The German propagandists had certainly done a convincing job. Cunning use of photography and newsreels gave the impression that the Luftwaffe was many times stronger than it really was. Nazi enthusiasts, who included the famous American pilot Charles

Lindbergh – the first to fly solo across the Atlantic – and Joseph Kennedy, the US Ambassador in London, thrilled to what they thought they saw. They reported gleefully to President Roosevelt in Washington that the RAF was outnumbered at least five to one and that Britain would fall in a matter of a few weeks if Goering's finest were to flock over the white cliffs of Dover towards London. The truth was that the Luftwaffe, created in 1935, was stretched, and always would be. True, it had some very capable commanders, fine aircraft and, by the summer of 1940, had experienced frontline fighting in Spain, Poland and France. But it was never as big or as efficient as Kennedy and Lindbergh either wanted or imagined it to be. Nor were many Luftwaffe commanders as happy with the idea of Britain's impending fall as these virulently anti-Semitic Americans. In fact, they felt much the same as Field Marshal Erhard Milch, another former First World War fighter pilot and one-time managing director of Deutsche Luft Hansa, who remarked, 'Chivalry is only possible between our two peoples. They are close to each other… I was born in the real old Saxon country where some of our words are the same as in English.'

There had, in fact, been a good deal of contact between senior German and British airmen during the 1930s, just as there had been a considerable amount of what would now be called 'technology transfer' – usually in the Luftwaffe's favour. Milch himself had regularly visited England. He was a great fan of the Hendon air shows and it was there, for example, that he learned about the theory of fuel injection for aero-engines from representatives of the Bristol Aircraft Company. The theory was later applied successfully to the Daimler-Benz engines which were to power large-scale production versions of Willy Messerschmitt's Bf 109 fighter, giving it an initial edge over the Spitfire in dives, climbs and high-altitude performance. Similarly, the Bf 109's clever wing slots, which helped endow it with such fine low-speed flying characteristics, had first been developed by the Handley Page company. Handley Page had been only too happy to demonstrate the workings of the device to Ernst Heinkel, from whose 1932 design, the He 64, Messerschmitt in turn took the idea. And as the Heinkel He 70 careered across English skies as a test-bed for Rolls-Royce's Kestrel and, later, Merlin engines, in Germany the prototype of the Junkers Ju 87 Stuka, like that of the Bf 109, took to the air powered by a Kestrel. Meanwhile, the handsome wooden hangars at Tangmere, where Spitfires and Hurricanes were to be serviced, had been built by German POWs in the First World War; they had done a fine job.

In 1937, Trenchard attended a banquet given by Goering in Berlin at the Charlottenburg Palace, where Goering told the founder of the RAF, 'It would be a pity if our two nations ever have to fight.' Trenchard told Goering not to underestimate the RAF. 'He's vulgar and coarse and brutal,' he said of the Reichsmarshal when he got back to England, 'but he's a great man.' German pilots flew three Bf 109s, complete with swastikas on their tails, to Hendon in 1937, and Milch came to visit Dowding and the Gloster Gladiator pilots of 65 Squadron, Hornchurch. He was particularly keen to see the latest RAF fighter gunsight, which Dowding kindly explained to him over the shoulder of young Bob Stanford Tuck, who in three years' time was to become a Spitfire ace.

When Milch returned to Berlin for a meeting with Hitler, he told him that the young British fighter pilots and cadets he had met were exactly like their German counterparts. He also told him that he had been seated next to Churchill at a dinner, and that Hitler's future nemesis had said to him, 'If only you would take the engines out of your aircraft and stick to gliding, we would feel happier.' To which Milch had replied, 'We should be only too pleased to do so if the Royal Navy would return to sailboats.' Hitler found this very funny. He also told Milch, 'You must rest assured that I shall always rely on England and try to co-operate with the English.'

At Cranwell, the RAF's training college, there was no great dislike, much less hatred, of Germany among cadets. Quite a few had been and were still to go on hiking holidays in the Bavarian Alps, where they would meet their Luftwaffe peers. Wilfrid Duncan Smith, later a very successful Spitfire pilot and the father of the recent Tory leader, recalls having a 'dust-up' with a 'young Nazi' over a girl in Innsbruck, but this is as far as hostilities usually went. In November 1938, when things were looking more serious, the cadets at Cranwell debated the motion, 'This House considers that an agreement with Germany is in the best interests of Great Britain and of the world at large'. It was defeated by thirty-six votes to thirty-four, but only apparently after one voice piped up to suggest that 'the persecution of the Jews precluded any decent-minded people from having anything to do with the Germans'.

By this time, the long-sighted Dowding more or less had his radar installations up and bleeping, along with his united air defence system with its inspired yet complex network of pilots, aircraft, airfields, radar, Observer Corps, barrage balloons and anti-aircraft batteries all threaded together by radio and telephone links. There remained some in government, Whitehall and the military who, uninformed or simply unthinking, were ready to suggest that Dowding was unwilling to fight when Nazi push really did come to Luftwaffe shove. What sort of commander was this that wanted to hold back all the time? Some sort of appeaser? Yet even while he had backed Neville Chamberlain, Prime Minister between 1937 and 1940, as he sought to win time for the RAF and for the Spitfire he had faithfully championed, Dowding had transformed Bentley Priory. From here he would now be able to direct his fighters as accurately as the times, technology and the competence of personnel in the air and on the ground allowed. What looked like the model of a kedgeree-for-breakfast English country house was, by the outbreak of war, the very model of a modern command centre.

Even in the late spring of 1940, it was uncertain whether or not Britain would stand up to Hitler. As MPs brayed for Chamberlain's resignation in May, it seemed likely that his successor would be Lord Halifax, who, if he had been appointed, might well have sued for peace. Halifax was not a closet Nazi; he was a peace-lover and genuinely believed that with the impending collapse of France it would be mad to continue the fight against Hitler. Indeed, when Winston Churchill, who was widely considered to be a war-hungry maverick, had been asked to form a government on the evening of 10 May, Halifax was planning a meeting with a Swedish businessman named Dahlerus, through whom he hoped to negotiate peace with Goering. The meeting took place on 20 May, the very day that General Heinz Guderian, the brilliant Blitzkrieg commander, drove his Panzers to the Channel and cut off the British Expeditionary Force. With the evacuation of British troops from Dunkirk looming, what hope could there possibly be now? In Westminster, there were MPs such as the anti-Communist and anti-Semitic Captain Ramsey who could see no reason whatsoever to fight Germany, our natural ally. At the opposite end of the political spectrum, the British Communist Party insisted that the war was a purely capitalist concern in which heroic workers should take no part.

Churchill and Dowding had their work cut out. Many of the new Prime Minister's colleagues felt that his moral argument in favour of war was largely irrelevant. What mattered was Britain's role as broker of the balance of world power. In a word, pragmatism. And yet Churchill, the great orator, won over the nation, or at least a large part of it, to the idea of total war with Germany. By July, Gallup polls showed Churchill's popularity rating among the public at up to 88 per cent. Victory at all costs, demanded the Prime Minister, stubborn as a bulldog. The public, if not the establishment, was behind him. Then, on 1 August 1940, Hitler issued his directive for an air offensive against Britain.

On 18 June, the 125th anniversary of the Battle of Waterloo, Churchill had made the speech that ensured the RAF's – and the Spitfire's – place in history. He told the House of Commons that 'The Battle of France is over. I expect that the Battle of Britain is about to begin.' He continued, 'The whole fury and might of the enemy must very soon be turned on us. Hitler knows that he will have to break us in this island or lose the war. If we can stand up to him, all Europe may be free, and the life of the world move forward into broad sunlit uplands. But, if we fail, then the whole world including the United States, including all that we have known and cared for, will sink into the abyss of a new Dark Age made more sinister, and perhaps more protracted, by the lights of perverted science. Let us, therefore, brace ourselves to our duties and so bear ourselves that, if the British Empire and its Commonwealth last for a thousand years, men will still say this was their finest hour.'

Even these inspiring words were a matter for contention in government circles. Duff Cooper, Churchill's Minister of Information, convinced the Prime Minister to repeat the speech on the wireless that evening. Churchill did so, puffing on a cigar throughout the live broadcast. Cooper could have kicked himself. He thought the Prime Minister sounded 'ghastly'. Cecil King, the newspaper magnate, thought Churchill's performance 'the poorest possible effort'. The King himself presumed that Winston, a man from whom the brandy bottle was never far away, was, to say the least, tired and emotional.

The Spitfire, meanwhile, had entered service with the Royal Air Force, some nine months after the Hawker Hurricane, on 4 August 1938, when 19 Squadron, Duxford, took delivery of K9789. Remarkably, this aircraft survived the war, only to be scrapped in 1945. The first RAF pilot to fly it was Squadron Leader Henry Cozens. His fighting career had begun in 1917 with the Sopwith Snipe biplane, Herbert Smith's improved Sopwith Camel, and was to end at the controls of Gloster Meteor and De Havilland Vampire jets. The Spitfire, Cozens said, was by far the best of all the aircraft he took to war.

By the end of the year, the RAF had two fully equipped Spitfire squadrons. On 3 September 1939, there were nine, based at Duxford, Hornchurch, Church Fenton, Catterick and Abbotschurch. To date, a total of 306 Mk Is had been delivered, although thirty-six had been written off during training. Each had cost about £9,500. The most expensive components were the hand-fabricated and finished fuselage at approximately £2,500, then the Rolls-Royce Merlin engine at £2,000, followed by the wings at £1,800 a pair, guns and undercarriage, both at £800 a shot, and the propeller at £350. The clock cost £2 10s 0d, and spark plugs for the Merlin were 8s 0d apiece.

Inevitably, RAF pilots were involved in many accidents as they transferred from the kindly biplane Tiger Moth and other trainers such as the Miles Magister and Master to the fast and powerful Spitfire. There was the view, or rather the lack of it on the ground, over the fighter's long nose, pointing up towards the sky; when taxiing, pilots had to wiggle the Spitfire from side to side to see where they were going. Coming in to land, all too many forgot to lower the wheels. Some found the undercarriage too narrow for comfort. Others had difficulty getting the machine to land; the Spitfire needs subtle, if firm, handling to stop it 'floating' above landing strips. Powered landings proved to be the answer, and then, with skill and experience, the Spitfire could be landed on the proverbial sixpence. Many pilots found themselves blacking out as they pulled turns tighter than they had ever imagined an aircraft being able to make. At 4g or 5g most pilots without pressure suits, no matter how fit, will find the skies blackening around their eyes. The Spitfire was quite able to pull 10g in turns, an absolutely astonishing feat for 1940. Imagine what that would mean to you as its pilot: if you weighed ten stone, at 10g your body would feel as if it weighed 100 stone.

The RAF sent doctors such as 'Doc' Horner to see how pilots were coping, and continued to do so throughout the war. In 1941, Wilfrid Duncan Smith was astonished to find Horner, by then fifty years old, flying into combat with him. Sitting resolutely on Duncan Smith's tail, Horner experienced combat, and thus aerobatics, to the full. When they landed at Hornchurch, Duncan Smith asked Horner why he had failed to fire when, for a good few seconds, he must have had a Bf 109 clearly in his sights. Horner answered, 'I didn't see any 109s. All I saw from start to finish was your tail and tail wheel. Funny how it keeps on going round and round.' Having sworn the Hippocratic oath, Horner had no intention of killing anyone, as his delightfully evasive answer made clear to the gun-happy young Spitfire pilot. The RAF was not wasteful of fighter pilots; it was keen, though, to understand the pressures its young men were under as they took to the air in ever faster and ever more demanding machines. (Many of the virgin pilots who went into battle in 1940 had a mere nine or so hours' experience with the Spitfire.)

Pilots, meanwhile, who had loved flying in their exquisitely aerobatic Hawker Fury biplanes found the cramped, enclosed cockpit of the Spitfire claustrophobic. They feared that scratches, condensation or oil streaks from the leaky Merlin engines across the Perspex canopies would impair their view in combat. At night they found the glare from the fire-spitting exhausts nearly blinded them, making landing a difficult and even dangerous manoeuvre. But whatever their initial fears, prejudices and failures, they were soon to love the Spitfire. She was their girl. Aerial totty. 'She was a perfect lady,' recalled Adolf 'Sailor' Malan, one of the leading Battle of Britain Spitfire aces. 'She had no vices. She was beautifully positive. You could dive till your eyes were popping out of your head… she would still answer to a touch.' Vices aside, all in all, the Spitfire was truly a winged spirit of ecstasy, a mechanical Lady Hamilton – no wonder they loved her. Most of all, Mitchell's and Shenstone's wing, the very signature of the Spitfire, was to get her pilots out of trouble time and time again. When in doubt, or with tracer whizzing behind your ears, the best thing to do was to turn as hard as you possibly could. No German aircraft could follow such manoeuvres, nor did you have to worry about the machine breaking up – it was immensely strong. Wilfrid Duncan Smith never forgot a visit the Supermarine test pilot Alex Henshaw made to RAF Hawarden, near William Gladstone's old home in Cheshire, while he was converting from a Miles Master to a Spitfire. 'By invitation, Alex gave a most excitingly executed flying display of aerobatics, both unique and difficult to perform, including a roll off the top of a loop immediately on taking off and a bunt [downward inverted outside half-loop] rolling out very close to the ground. He started the bunt no higher than 1,200 feet or so. Incredible.'

The Spitfires of 74 Squadron made the machine's first kills, over the River Medway, Kent, on 6 September 1939. Unfortunately, the enemy proved to be two Hurricanes from 56 Squadron. An inquiry highlighted a fault in the RAF's fighter control system and the pilots were exonerated. This then led to the installation of IFF (Identification Friend or Foe) equipment, a form of transponder, which was to save many lives from 'friendly fire'.

The honour of Fighter Command was restored on 16 October, when 603 Squadron shot down two Junkers Ju 88s of 1/KG 30 led by Hauptmann Helmuth Pohle over Rosyth by the Firth of Forth. The Germans had been hoping to attack HMS *Hood*, the battlecruiser later sunk by the *Bismarck*. The *Hood* was elsewhere that day, but the Ju 88s did manage a crack at the cruisers HMS *Southampton* and HMS *Edinburgh* before the fighters arrived. Spitfires based in England made their first kill when 41 Squadron, from Catterick, shot down a Heinkel He 111 off Whitby.

These were skirmishes, and there were to be many more, before the Battle of Britain proper. The period in between was known as the Phoney War. Nothing much appeared to happen in Britain, but the Germans were very much on the advance, invading Norway in April 1940, and the Low Countries and France the following month. On 10 May 1940, Spitfires finally flew across the Channel, their pilots coming up against Luftwaffe fighters for the first time in the form of Bf 109s and twin-engined Bf 110s. This was the beginning of what Churchill was to refer to as the Battle of France; this was also when Dowding put his foot down, refusing to send his precious Spitfires to bases in France. 'I believe,' he had written in the tenth and final terse paragraph of his memorandum of 18 April addressed to the Under Secretary for Air, 'that if an adequate fighter force is kept in this country, if the Fleet remains in being, and if the Home Forces are suitably organized to resist invasion, we should be able to carry on the war single-handed for some time, if not indefinitely. But, if the Home Defence Force is drained away in desperate attempts to remedy the situation in France, defeat in France will lead to the final, complete and irremediable defeat of this Country.' Churchill, for all his love of France, had to agree. The army complained, calling Dowding's pilots 'the Brylcreem Boys' – all style, in other words, and no substance, and never there to help when help was needed. Nevertheless, sixty-seven valuable Spitfires were lost over France, most of them in the attempt to prevent the Luftwaffe from bombing the evacuation beaches at Dunkirk.

The pilots who fought over France and survived had, however, learned a few useful tips on how to take on the Messerschmitts. The trick was to get the fitters back at base to 'harmonize' the Browning machine-guns so that their combined fire met their target in one concentrated burst just 250 yards ahead of the wings, instead of the official 400 yards. This encouraged squadron leaders to advise their pilots to get in fast and close to the enemy before firing, and then to dart away. It was a surer way of making a kill than flying elegantly and trying a polite deflection shot as if aiming at a pheasant. Judging how far to fire ahead of a target moving at 300 mph or more across your gunsights was a very fine art indeed. Few, in fact, succeeded. Most of the kills made during the Battle of Britain, and throughout the Second

Gun camera footage taken from a Spitfire Mk I of 609 Squadron as its pilot attacked a Heinkel He III bomber on 25 September 1940.

World War, were made by aces. They were aces because they were good shots. And they were good shots because they came in close and fast, and then climbed away, ready either to dive at the next target or to fly home. Far too many inexperienced pilots would follow a 'wounded' enemy aircraft to see what happened to it, and then find a Bf 109, or later a Focke-Wulf Fw 190, on their tail. Actually, most would never even see it before they too went down in flames.

RAF pilots had also learned that the pattern in which they had been taught to fly, in 'Vics', or threes, was folly. The greenest pilot was given the job of tailing two more senior pilots as they hunted for action and was often pounced on without the leading pair even noticing until it was too late. Luftwaffe fighter pilots patrolled instead in two close-coupled pairs, known as a 'finger four', which you can recreate very easily using your own hands. As soon as the enemy, or *Indianen*, were spotted, the German cowboys would split into two pairs, the second aircraft in each pair following his leader precisely and watching out for him as he went into attack. The system worked extremely well. It was far from an overnight conversion, but all except the most dunderheaded RAF pilots eventually adopted the German tactics.

Some of the best Battle of Britain pilots had been crackshots in the field before joining up, and the image of the young toff Spitfire pilot has always been hard for the RAF to shake off. They made up by no means the majority of Spitfire pilots in the summer of 1940, yet they undoubtedly produced a colourful impact and were instrumental in helping to create the myth of the insouciant, unflappable sort of chap who, ever since, is assumed to have been the archetypal Spitfire pilot. Fourteen Battle of Britain fighter squadrons, a quarter of the total, came from the RAAF (Royal

Auxiliary Air Force), founded by Lord Trenchard in 1925. These squadrons were indeed the haunt of devil-may-care, hunting, fishing and shooting public-school types. Lord Edward Grosvenor, a direct descendant of William I, who had successfully invaded England in 1066, formed 601 (County of London) Squadron, from fellow members of his exclusive London club, White's in St James's. It would have been impolite, and simply not on, to turn him down. One of the poshest of Battle of Britain squadrons, 601 flew Hurricanes in 1940. Yet it was the RAFVR (Royal Air Force Volunteer Reserve), formed in 1936, that supplied a third of all Battle of Britain pilots. Drawn from across the social spectrum, they took to the air as pilot sergeants and were not expected to darken the doors of officers' messes.

Others making up this elite included, of course, the RAF's regular pilots, those who had joined straight from school and passed through the service's own college, Cranwell, established in 1933. They included such natural English gentlemen as Peter Townsend, who very nearly married Princess Margaret after the war, and Robert Roland Stanford Tuck. In 1932, 'Lucky Tuck' had left St Dunstan's School, a fifteenth-century foundation that moved to salubrious Catford, south-east London, towards the end of the nineteenth century. After a spell sailing the world with the Merchant Navy, he joined the RAF in 1935 and flew Gladiators with 65 Squadron before being selected as one of the first Spitfire pilots in late 1938. He went into action, with 92 Squadron, Croydon, on 23 May 1940. Within the next twenty-four hours, he had shot down a brace of Bf 110Cs, a pair of Dornier Do 17s and a Bf 109E. In June, he flew a captured Bf 109E at Farnborough in mock dogfights with a Spitfire Mk II. It taught him, he said, to get inside the minds, and hands, of Messerschmitt pilots – and to shoot them

Robert Stanford Tuck in the cockpit of the Hurricane he flew when CO of 257 Squadron in 1940 and 1941: he much preferred the Spitfire.

down. On 18 August 1940, he destroyed a Junkers Ju 88A and then lost half his propeller and gallons of oil and ethylene glycol attacking another. He bailed out and landed in the grounds of Lord Cornwallis's estate at Horsmonden, Kent, in time for tea with his lordship.

Stanford Tuck clocked up around 1,000 hours in Spitfires before being asked to take over command of 257 Squadron, a Hurricane Mk I outfit whose luck had been hard and whose morale was low. 'After the Spit,' he said, 'it [the Hurricane] was like a flying brick… a great, lumbering farmyard stallion compared with a dainty and gentle thoroughbred… nearly broke my heart, because things seemed tough enough without having to take on 109s in a heavy great kite like this.' On 15 September, 'Battle of Britain Day', when the RAF was finally to have its wings torn off for good, Stanford Tuck led a wing comprising 257 and two other Hurricane squadrons – and they did their bit, with honours. He positively encouraged wayward flying to keep the enemy guessing, and lively banter over the radio to keep spirits up. He was also popular with his ground crews. As former Leading Aircraftsman John Ryder recalled many years later, 'Tuck always took a real interest in his ground crews and never had that "toffee nose" attitude that some pilots displayed towards us. He gave us all consideration and confidence.'

Shot down again over the Thames, and rescued by a coal barge, Tuck took command in July 1941 of Duxford Wing, now flying a Mk V Spitfire, powered by the latest, uprated version of the Merlin and armed with two 20-mm Hispano cannon and four Brownings. In October 1941, by now decorated with the DFC and two bars, and the DSO – all of them 'down to luck' – he was shipped off to the United States, with 'Sailor' Malan and Group Captain Harry Broadhurst, to train US fighter pilots. While there he met Rita Hayworth, who taught him to jive. Back in England in time for Christmas, Tuck took on the Biggin Hill Wing, comprising four Spitfire squadrons, and 264 Squadron, a nightfighter unit equipped with Boulton Paul Defiants. His target on

28 January 1942 was an alcohol distillery at Hesdin, Normandy. After destroying the target, Tuck pressed on with an attack against electricity power lines, an army truck and a freight locomotive in a valley leading towards the heavy flak installations at Boulogne. Then bang, down he came. Astonishingly, one of the last bursts of cannon fire from his Spitfire split the barrel of the anti-aircraft gun that had brought him down. This was pure luck, although his captors thought it was all but unbelievable marksmanship.

The Germans were suitably impressed by the numbers of swastikas, marking 'kills', painted under the canopy of Tuck's Mk V. They took him off in a lorry to St Omer, where in the First World War Dowding had led his fighter squadron, to see Oberst Adolf Galland, the great Luftwaffe ace who was very soon to be the youngest general in the German armed forces, commanding all Luftwaffe fighters. Galland invited Tuck to join him and his officers for dinner. There was plenty to drink, and the pilots chatted about fellow aces on both sides as if 'they were old chums temporarily absent'. 'I am very glad that you are not badly hurt,' Galland said to Tuck, shaking hands without giving a Heil Hitler salute, at the end of the evening, 'and that you will not have to risk your life anymore.' It proved the start of an enduring friendship between the two men. They had, in fact, met at least once before, in the air, during the course of 1941. In one dogfight, Galland had shot down Tuck's wingman, and Tuck had reciprocated. Years later, Stanford Tuck's sons were to stand beside the grave of General der Jagdflieger Galland as his coffin was lowered and the funeral rites were read. The ghost of their charming and gallant father no doubt stood alongside too.

Tuck was sent to Stalag Luft III prison camp at Sagan, near Berlin. Here he was to have been one of the 200 RAF pilots who were going to have a bash at escaping through 'Harry', a 400-foot tunnel leading under the wires. This was the famous 'Great Escape'. Of the seventy-six POWs who made it through the tunnel, only three got away. Fifty of those rounded up were summarily executed by the Gestapo. 'Lucky Tuck' had been transferred that very morning to Belaria, another camp a few miles away. He finally escaped during a forced march in January 1945 as the Red Army closed in on Germany's eastern front. During a stop, he hid under a pile of straw with Zbishek Kustrzynski, a Polish pilot, and together they trekked east. When they met the Russians, they were sent to Odessa and brought back to Southampton on board the *Duchess of Richmond*, arriving on 26 March 1945.

Shortly after the war had ended, Tuck, now married to his childhood sweetheart and back with Spitfires at Tangmere, watched a C-47 transport plane land one lunchtime. On board were two top-scoring Luftwaffe aces, one of whom had flown the Me 262 jet fighter in the very last few months of hostilities and was wanted for questioning on technical matters by both the Americans and the British. This former Bf 109 pilot was the future General Gunther Rall, who in 1955 was to be one of the founders of the Bundesluftwaffe, the Federal Republic of Germany's Air Force. He had 275 kills and a Knight's Cross, with oak leaves and crossed swords, to his name. The other was Stuka ace Hans-Ulrich Rudel.

Rall recalls that Stanford Tuck approached them, saluted in the very relaxed manner Spitfire pilots used, and asked, 'Have you gentlemen had lunch?' 'Not for the past three months,' Rall replied. 'This was the first time I had been treated with respect in as many months,' he later told me from his fine old Bavarian hunting lodge, set like an eagle's nest above Bad Reichenhall. 'Stanford Tuck called us gentlemen. This was a surprise. As was the lunch with beer, the hot baths and clean blankets in the huts. That experience… taught me what might seem obvious to you, that wars, idiotic things, might be caused by weak or morally cretinous people, but they are fought and endured by very decent ones.'

Decent Bob Stanford Tuck retired from the RAF in 1949 and took up mushroom farming in Kent. He died, aged three score years and ten, in 1987. In 1982, and rather to his surprise, he was told that his score as a fighter pilot had just been raised from twenty-nine to thirty. A German bomber that he had thought was a 'probable' had been discovered in Kent. 'Must have been a lucky shot,' he remarked.

If Stanford Tuck was in many ways the apotheosis of the Spitfire pilot, he was in many other ways untypical. He was even looked down on as a bit of a show-off when he set the trend for recording each of his kills with a swastika below his Spitfire's canopy. I have told his story because it is one of a spirited, skilled, much liked and decidedly fortunate man. But one in five Battle of Britain pilots, who wanted to fight Hitler, or simply to fly Spitfires, were drawn from much further afield than Catford. They came from across North America, the British Empire and Commonwealth and Nazi-occupied Europe. In the summer of 1940, Poles fought alongside Czechs, New Zealanders, Australians, Canadians, South Africans, Free French, Belgians and Rhodesians. The first American to die fighting for Britain in the Second World War was a Battle of Britain pilot; he was twenty-nine-year-old Pilot Officer Billy Fiske, an ice hockey star and supercharged Bentley-driving playboy banker and film producer, who had married Rose, the former Countess of Warwick, in 1938 and so qualified for membership of Edward Grosvenor's 601 Squadron based at Tangmere.

Fiske survived the best part of a month in action. His legend, however, encouraged other Americans to follow. By August 1941, US pilots had formed three RAF 'Eagle' Squadrons, 71, 121 and 133, flying Spitfires and Hurricanes. Altogether, 244 US pilots flew for the Eagles before the squadrons were merged into the USAAF in September 1942. In all, 2,353 British and 574 pilots from overseas flew in the Battle of Britain; of these, 544 were killed in the battle itself, and a further 791 were to die in action before the war ended with Japan's surrender in August 1945.

A Spitfire Mk IA of 19 Squadron is rearmed at Fowlmere, Cambridgeshire, in September 1940.

The Battle of Britain was officially fought from 10 July until 31 October 1940. The RAF flew nineteen Spitfire and twenty-five Hurricane squadrons. There were six further squadrons of Blenheim night-fighters and two squadrons of Defiants, which, after a brief moment of glory over Dunkirk, were also switched to night operations. On any particular day, Fighter Command could scramble a maximum of approximately 600 Spitfires and Hurricanes. They were faced on the other side of the Channel by the Luftwaffe's Luftflotte 2, commanded by General 'Smiling Albert' Kesselring, and Luftflotte 3, under General Hugo Sperrle, which, on an average day, could field up to 1,000 bombers including single-engined Ju 87 Stukas, 650 Bf 109s and 160 Bf 110s. Between 10 July and 31 October, 352 Spitfires were lost and 565 Hurricanes. Although Hurricanes shot down more enemy aircraft in total, in terms of the ratio of kills, honours were pretty much even between the two British fighters.

In August 1940, Jeffrey Quill left off testing new Spitfires and flew in action for nineteen days with 65 Squadron, shooting down two Bf 109s. He recommended two important alterations to the aircraft as a result. One was to improve all-round vision by slight changes to the shape of the canopy; the other was to fit far stronger, all-metal ailerons to the wings. In very necessary steep dives, Quill had discovered for himself the way in which the Spitfire's controls became uncomfortably heavy as the pilot attempted to pull the nose back up. The canvas-covered ailerons ballooned when the aircraft dived. Once the new ailerons were fitted, the problem was essentially solved. Quill's further suggestion that a meter indicating how many rounds of ammunition were left in the guns was not adopted.

Just before the modifications could be made, the RAF began to turn the tide. On 18 August it destroyed sixty-nine enemy aircraft and damaged a further thirty-one, while losing thirty-four of its own aircraft with thirty-nine damaged. RAF fighter pilots had reached what they and their rivals across the Channel saw as the magic kill ratio of 2:1. Reports of 'definite' and 'probable' kills were inevitably exaggerated by pilots on both sides in the thick of battle. Dogfights and other skirmishes were fast, furious and only very rarely lasted more than a few minutes. It could be very hard to follow the action. At one point in August, the Air Minister had the nerve to caution Dowding, 'There are serious doubts about your pilots' claims.' 'Stuffy' replied, unsmilingly, 'If the German claims were correct, they'd be in England by now.'

At this point, the RAF's fighter pilots needed above all to maintain both their own momentum and whatever hit rate it was that they were really scoring. Every last available Hurricane and Spitfire was hurled into the tumultuous fray. The factories down below in Southampton, Yeovil and Castle Bromwich were doing their bit, especially now that Churchill's favourite business tycoon, Lord Beaverbrook, was in charge of production, turning out impressive numbers of Spitfires, ever more of them paid for by companies, guilds, corporations and private individuals. But on 18 August the RAF had formed a very thin blue line indeed.

Churchill had driven out to the RAF's Uxbridge headquarters that afternoon with his Chief of Staff, General Ismay, to see for himself how they were coping. When they left in the car for Chequers, Churchill said to Ismay, 'Don't speak to me; I have never been so moved.' A few minutes later, he leaned over and said: 'Never in the field of human conflict has so much been owed by so many to so few.' Two days later, Churchill used the words in a speech to the House of Commons. One fighter pilot is said to have quipped: 'Careful, chaps, the PM has seen our mess bill.'

While Churchill did his brilliant thing in the Commons and on the wireless, Dowding and in particular the tireless New Zealand-born Air Vice Marshal Keith Park, who was in charge of 11 Fighter Group and thus the defence of London and the South-East, utilized every last bit of intelligence to direct their pilots at an enemy who was now flying a prodigious 1,500 sorties a day over the Channel. Strikes by Stuka and Bf 110 fighter-bombers on RAF airfields and radar stations were, fortunately for the hard-pressed Fighter Command, rarely followed through. (Although neither Dowding nor Park could have known this at the time, Hitler was on the verge of ordering Goering to direct his bombers on London, saving Britain's airfields from destruction.) In his desire for first-hand information, Park, a beanpole of a man (untypically for a fighter pilot, he was 6′ 5″ tall), flew his personal Hurricane into the fray to see what was going on and what was needed to win. He would fly from airfield to airfield, dressed in an immaculate, old-fashioned white flying suit, finding out what his men wanted and boosting morale.

After one last burst of raids on airfields, the Luftwaffe moved on to attack London. The big raid came on 7 September with an aerial flotilla of 348 bombers and 617 fighters making its way towards the city. The death rate among the civilian population was horrific. And yet, as Peter Townsend records, people swam and boated in Hyde Park's Serpentine and asked what the score was in the air battle overhead, 'as if it had been a Test match'. After raids on Cardiff, the local St Mellons Golf Club issued an amended list of rules: 'A ball moved by enemy action may be replaced… a ball lying in a crater may be dropped… A player whose stroke is affected by the simultaneous explosion of a bomb… or by machine-gun fire may play another ball… penalty one stroke.' In certain ways, the British were nothing like the Germans.

Dowding and Park were able to recoup their strength. By the time the Luftwaffe again struck specifically against the RAF on 15 September, days ahead of the intended start of Hitler's Operation Sealion, Fighter Command had more pilots and aircraft than it had started out with in July. (Beaverbrook had telephoned Park eagerly every evening to find out what replacements he needed. Thanks to 'The Beaver', Park said, 11 Group never lacked for aircraft.) On that day, Churchill was again watching over Park's shoulder in the Ops Room at Uxbridge as he directed his fighters with great skill. If Park was at all nervous, it was because he was unsure what Air Vice Marshal Trafford Leigh-Mallory was up to with his 12 Group, which was flying a rather different battle to Park's and Dowding's.

Leigh-Mallory, whose elder brother George had frozen to death in an attempt to be the first man to climb Everest, championed what was known as the Big Wing. This was the tin-legged ace Douglas Bader's great idea. He thought it made little sense to send in small number of fighters, guerrilla-style, against the vast aerial flotillas the Luftwaffe was now launching across the Channel. What was needed was wheeling flocks, or wings, of fighters hurled into the German formations. In the event, the Big Wing was not a great success – it took far too long to organize in the air – although it did the RAF a service in that it reminded Luftwaffe pilots that, despite what their political overlords and intelligence officers were telling them, Fighter Command was flexing ever more muscle as the Battle of Britain climbed to its zenith in mid-September.

For all the adrenaline and blood they had expended, most RAF pilots were still in love with flight. Before he recovered and flew on his final, fatal Battle of Britain Spitfire sortie, Pilot Officer Bill Millington wrote home from Croydon General Hospital to his parents in Australia, 'Flying has meant more than a livelihood… the companionship of men and boys with similar interests, the intoxication of speed, the rush of air, and the pulsating beat of the motor awakes some answering cord deep down, which is indescribable.' As it was, the Luftwaffe's nerve finally cracked on the evening of 15 September. It had lost fifty-six aircraft on that fine late summer day: no matter how many machines it put into the air, in wave upon wave, Spitfires and Hurricanes were waiting to pounce. The day had begun with Air Vice Marshal Park forgetting to buy his wife a birthday present. When he apologized, she said that a bag of German aircraft would make up for his understandable lapse of memory. He had, after all, been living on his wits and nerves day in, day out for the past five months.

At 11 a.m., the piping voice of Corporal Daphne Griffiths, reporting from Rye, could be heard at Stanmore and relayed to Uxbridge: 'Hullo Stanmore, hostile six is now at fifteen miles. Height 15,000.' Corporal Griffiths's report of fifty enemy aircraft soon turned into hundreds, flown in no fewer than 1,300 sorties. A bomb hit Buckingham Palace. A Dornier crashed into the glass roof of Victoria station, its crew bailing out over the Oval cricket ground. Douglas Bader, whirling in a Big Wing over Battersea power station, thrilled to 'the finest shambles I've ever been in'. In his private armoured train, parked in a siding at Boulogne, Goering listened to a report from Hauptmann Bernd von Brauchitsch: 'They must be reaching the end of their resources. Today's assault should complete the operation.' Goering, of course, was told what his officers assumed he wanted to hear, and not the truth. It did not help. 'They', as it turned out that day, were the Luftwaffe, not

Fighter Command. Not to be left out, Bomber Command celebrated that evening with heavy raids on Antwerp and Le Havre, flying into the fray as if the Luftwaffe had lost every last one of its fighters.

On 21 September, Hitler put Operation Sealion on permanent hold. The Battle of Britain was effectively over. Adolf Galland reported to Adolf Hitler on the 27th, expressing his 'greatest admiration for the enemy across the water'. The Führer did not disagree. He explained to his young fighter commander that his great regret was that he had 'failed to bring the German and English peoples together'. However, he would, of course, carry on bombing them and then launch rocket-powered weapons at them. By the end of the Second World War, 60,000 British civilians had been killed, and by the time Hitler put a gun to his own head, more than ten times that number of German civilians had died.

The Spitfires had done their bit for Britain. Remarkably, the Luftwaffe failed to attack the Spitfire factory at Southampton until 24 September. The raid that day killed 100 Supermarine staff. A second raid two days later killed another thirty and put the plant temporarily out of production. The Westland factory at Yeovil, which had been producing Spitfires for some months, was badly hit on 30 September. The Castle Bromwich factory, however, was out of range to all but the most determined night-raiders: it was never hit, and after the war Jaguar cars were built there.

The Spitfire itself had come through 1940 with flying colours. It had bewitched both those who flew it, the British public and the pilots of the Luftwaffe. Famously, when Adolf Galland was asked by Hermann Goering what he wanted most to fight the RAF, he replied 'Spitfires'. Spitfire squadrons were made up of all sorts of young men, many of them teenagers, although the word did not exist then. Most pilots were given a schoolboyish nickname. In Wilfrid Duncan Smith's wartime reminiscences, *Spitfire into Battle*, there seems to be one on every second page: 'Polly', 'Sadie', 'Bitters', 'Zulu', 'Ginger', 'Streak', 'Peggy', 'Jacko', 'Warbie', 'Smidge', and, my favourites, 'Mushroom' and 'Sheep'. There were those for whom the *Sporting Life* was all you ever needed to read, and those for whom the fight against Hitler was as personal as it was philosophical. These pilots came from an extraordinary range of backgrounds and nationalities. They included former public- and grammar-school boys, a cocktail shaker from the Dorchester Hotel, regular RAF pilots, volunteers, sergeants and officers, and those who lied about their age and even got away with being less than the statutory 5′ 5″ tall. If they all had any one thing in common, then it was perhaps that they were fighting against a bully, against an enemy that had the nerve to assume that the British, and their allies, would ever want to become part of Adolf Hitler's chillingly authoritarian Reich. This was cause enough to scramble for the cockpit of a Spitfire.

But the Spitfire owed its success, both then and later, to others besides those who flew it into battle and who developed and built it: the men and women of the ATA, the Air Transport Auxiliary. There is a particularly cherishable and wonderfully romantic image of Diana Barnato-Walker climbing into the cockpit of a Spitfire. Her job, like those of her ATA colleagues, was to deliver Spitfires, among many other makes and models of aircraft, from the factories to RAF airfields. If Barnato-Walker had been able to get her own way, she would, of course, have been a combat pilot. There were many women who wanted to be. Lady Mary Bailey, the mother of Jim Bailey, a Defiant pilot and later the publisher of the anti-apartheid magazine *Drum* in South Africa, was married to

Air Transport Auxiliary pilot Diana Barnato-Walker climbs into the cockpit of a Spitfire Mk IX at RAF Hamble in 1945.

Sir Abe Bailey. Sir Abe had financed Churchill through his 'wilderness years' before Hitler decided to invade Poland on 1 September 1939. Mary was a pioneering pilot herself, having done much to open up commercial air routes from England to South Africa in the early 1930s, flying a De Havilland Moth. She wrote time and again to Churchill, Bailey told me, demanding to be made a Spitfire pilot.

It was not to be. Diana Barnato-Walker, who had been born in 1918, did fly Spitfires, but not during the Battle of Britain as she would have dearly liked. She had been born for the role. Her father was the millionaire and three-times-married Le Mans-winning Bentley racing driver, Woolf 'Babe' Barnato, grandson of

Isaac Isaacs, a Cockney shopkeeper, and son of Barnett Isaacs, who changed his family name to Barnato, sailed to South Africa and made his fortune in diamond mining. Barnett Barnato disappeared over the side of the ship bringing him back, with Woolf, to England. Woolf went on to finance W. O. Bentley and, when the great motor engineer was bought out by Rolls-Royce in 1931, Barnato continued to invest in the company that was soon to develop the Merlin.

Diana was presented by her father with a 95-mph, 4¼-litre Park Ward Bentley on her twenty-first birthday. But she wanted to do something her famous father had not done – fly. She went solo, in six hours, in a Tiger Moth at Brooklands, Surrey. This was just before war was declared. Diana volunteered as a Red Cross nurse, but was quickly accepted into the ATA. Here she joined the likes of the pioneering aviatrix Amy Johnson and Lettice Curtis, the first woman to fly a four-engined Avro Lancaster bomber. Diana recalls flying with a motley crew that included, at one time or another, a bookmaker, a conjuror, a one-eyed, one-armed fifty-year-old Great War veteran named Stuart Keith-Jopp and 'Poppy' Fairweather, who calculated time and distance in the air by the number of cigarettes he smoked: one cigarette equalled seven minutes' flying. Still, this was perhaps a better method than that employed by Lady Mary Bailey on her way south through Africa: she simply landed, got out and asked where she was. To be fair, she had hoped to learn some trigonometry from her son Jim before she took off; Jim explained that he wasn't doing 'trig' until next term, so Lady Mary took off from Oxfordshire to Africa without it.

The ATA was the brainchild of thirty-two-year-old Gerard d'Erlanger, director of the pre-war British Airways. Convinced during 1938 that war with Germany was inevitable, d'Erlanger envisaged a time ahead when many of the best commercial pilots would be banned from flying. Not only would many of them be too old for the RAF, but the Air Ministry would be sure to put a halt to most commercial flying. What would be needed, d'Erlanger believed, were flights to fetch and carry political mail and military dispatches, aircraft that could serve as ambulances and pilots who could deliver fighting machines from factories to RAF airfields. The idea received a highly favourable reply from Harold Balfour, Under Secretary for Air, and the Director General of Civil Aviation, Sir Francis Shelmerdine. They suggested d'Erlanger might like the job. He took it.

The timing was tight. The ATA was formed on the day war broke out. The first thirty recruits were men. Were women up to the job? Not according to C. G. Grey, editor of *The Aeroplane*, who thundered: 'We quite agree... that there are millions of women in the country who could do useful jobs in war. But the trouble is that so many of them insist on wanting to do jobs which they are quite incapable of doing. The menace is the woman who thinks that she ought to be flying in a high-speed bomber when she really has not the intelligence to scrub the floor of a hospital properly, or who wants to nose around as an Air Raid Warden and yet can't cook her husband's dinner.'

Not surprisingly, Pauline Gower, a twenty-nine-year-old commercial pilot with over 2,000 hours' flying, disagreed. She championed the cause of women joining the ATA and, beginning with eight women pilots ferrying De Havilland Tiger Moth trainers, became d'Erlanger's right-hand woman, holding the position throughout the war. Her female pilots, who adored her, were first based at Hatfield near the De Havilland factory. Among them were at least one grandmother, a ballet dancer, an architect, an actress, an ice-hockey champion and a typist, and they flew open-cockpit Tiger Moths to Scotland in the depth of the bitter winter of 1939–40. Despite their obvious prowess, old attitudes died hard: women, it was said, were not up to flying powerful machines such as the Spitfire. And so, even while their services were very much needed, female ATA pilots had to wait until after the Battle of Britain to fly Mitchell's wonderful little lady. They finally flew Spitfires, from Southampton, in September 1941, and as the war progressed they took to the air in pretty much anything with wings and an engine, from Spitfires and Hurricanes and Tempests and Typhoons to Lancasters and Flying Fortresses. They flew without radios and with empty guns and faced the constant threat of attack by marauding German aircraft or friendly fire from ack-ack batteries down below.

American women sailed the U-boat-infested Atlantic to join the ATA. Female pilots were given equal pay with their male colleagues in 1943, and in 1944 they got to fly across the Channel. Diana Barnato-Walker was the first to do so; she flew to Brussels in a Spitfire following another Spitfire flown by her second husband, Wing Commander Derek Walker, who died eighteen months later when he crashed his P-51D Mustang at Hendon. (Diana's first husband, Squadron Leader Humphrey Gilbert, had died in a Spitfire crash in 1942.) Barnato-Walker certainly impressed even such hard-bitten Spitfire aces as Wilfrid Duncan Smith. As the newly appointed Wing Commander at North Weald, Essex, in 1942, he 'had a shock one dismal afternoon when a Beaufighter crept in to land while the airfield was closed due to severe bad weather. The intrepid pilot turned out to be Diana Barnato, a pilot in the Air Transport Auxiliary. Looking very beautiful in her immaculate uniform, she ran a comb through her hair before climbing out of the aircraft to tell me that she was short of fuel and had had a very rough flight through the thunderstorms. Not the least put out by the weather or the fact that she had made an emergency landing, her only concern was not to be a nuisance or disturb anyone. I discovered later that she had flown a considerable distance and that her Beaufighter had not been equipped with any radio or navigational aids while she carried out the flight with only her map and the aircraft's compass.'

In flying to wartime Brussels, Barnato-Walker had set a precedent. Soon afterwards, female ATA pilots began to fly all the way to Germany. In the last months of the war, they delivered Meteor jets. On VJ Day, an ATA pilot, Monique Agazarian, flew a Spitfire low along the length of Piccadilly. This was to be the end, for some years, of women flying RAF service aircraft. There was, though, a happy postscript. One evening in 1963, in the officers' mess of RAF Middleton St George, Teesside, Wing Commander John Severgne asked Barnato-Walker if she might like to fly a Lightning jet fighter. On 26 August, with the permission of the Ministry of Defence, Diana blasted through the sound barrier on her way to Mach 1.65, or 1,262 mph. Her father, her late husbands and Pauline Gower would have been impressed. Gower herself died tragically in 1947 soon after giving birth to twin boys. Altogether, twenty women ATA pilots died in service. They had been the very 'Few' indeed.

Women had also joined the ATA as mechanics. In fact, very many Spitfires from the Battle of Britain onwards were built by women. In the autumn of 2005, the Science Museum in London put on a fine exhibition of Spitfires and how they were built. Among the many photographs in the care of the museum are those

Joan Lisle at a drawing board at the Castle Bromwich factory.

showing young women at work in the vast Castle Bromwich factory. Here are best friends Edna Pugh and Kitty Moore assembling the internal wing structure of a Spitfire. Here is nineteen-year-old Janet May, a former draper's assistant from Leicester, fabricating a fuselage. And here is a photograph showing Joan Lisle, a doppelgänger for John Betjeman's Miss Joan Hunter-Dunn, busy at a Castle Bromwich drawing board. Joan started work there during the Phoney War. She had previously worked for Austin at Longbridge. As well as working on the development of the Spitfire, she was a principal member of the factory's amateur dramatics society and organized the annual pantomine. The story of the Spitfire as it rose to prominence in 1940 is that of Joan Lisle and others like her as well as of Dowding, Park, Leigh-Mallory, Stanford Tuck and the 'Few'.

CHAPTER III

SURVIVAL OF
THE FITTEST

RHUBARBS and Circuses. Put together, these words, seemingly drawn at random from the dictionary, sound like the title of a popular children's television series. For RAF fighter pilots flying through the winter of 1940–41, they spelled anything but child's play. A Rhubarb, in RAF lingo, meant a low-level attack on railway marshalling yards, on bridges, barges, lorries, flak batteries, on anything really that could be construed as a legitimate enemy target through the gunsights of a pair of fighters sweeping across the French coast in search of trouble. The targets were, in fact, largely secondary to the primary aim of chivvying Luftwaffe fighters into the air, taking them on and, hopefully, reducing their numbers. Flying a Rhubarb, even in a Spitfire, was not much fun. Low flying meant flak from well dug-in gun emplacements, and plenty of it, as experienced pilots such as Bob Stanford Tuck were to discover soon enough, to their cost.

A Circus was a bombing mission involving a small cluster of bombers accompanied on daylight raids over the Low Countries

A trainee pilot takes off in a Spitfire Mk II at 61 OTU, Rednal, Staffordshire, in 1942.

and France by Big Wings of fighters. The aim, again, was to lure the Luftwaffe's fighters into action and, in doing so, to keep RAF fighter pilots up to the mark. However, a Circus was not much fun either; Spitfires designed to fly at 350 mph were forced to cruise alongside slow, low-flying bombers, and their pilots knew that they might be bounced at any time by high-flying Messerschmitts hiding, like birds of prey, in the glare of the sun.

The war had changed after the Battle of Britain. It was now widely considered unlikely that Britain would be invaded. Attacked, yes, and it would be right through the war, and latterly by V1 and V2 rockets; stamped over by jackboots, no. It was time, then, for the RAF to take on an offensive rather than a defensive role, and for fighter pilots and their winged machines to meld into an altogether bigger picture than the one they had painted in white contrails against blue skies in the summer of 1940. Not surprisingly, Dowding, the master of defence, was put out to grass, while Park was moved on to other, exotic theatres of war. It was time, too, for the Spitfire itself to grow up, to put on a bit of beef, to widen its scope of operation, and to confront some deadly new enemies.

Over the next five years, the Spitfire was to become a rather different aircraft. It grew heavier and more powerful. It sprouted bigger and more devastating guns. It learned to carry rockets and bombs. It flew high and falcon-fast, painted blue or an odd dusty pink, in its ever-expanding role as a highly successful photo-reconnaissance plane. A PR Mk IX of 542 Squadron brought back the famous photographs showing the German dams on the Ruhr breached by the Merlin-engined Lancasters of Guy Gibson's 617 'Dambuster' Squadron on 12 May 1943. The raid might not have greatly damaged Hitler's war effort, but in terms of raising British morale those photographs taken from a Spitfire that swept down from altitude to buzz the dams were gold dust.

The Spitfire flew from its cradle in England, and became a star of the campaign to drive the Axis powers from Sicily and then the Italian peninsula. It stretched its wings across the Soviet Union from the time of the Battle of Stalingrad, with red stars painted on fuselage and tail. From 1942 to 1945, it fought from and over deserts, jungles, Robinson Crusoe islands and distant oceans. It found a roost as far away from Southampton as Darwin in Australia's Northern Territory. It found itself attacked by Yugoslav fighters, who were meant to be on the side of the Allies, after the uncon-ditional German surrender in May 1945. It flew, as the Seafire, with the Royal Navy from the decks of aircraft carriers in the Mediterranean and Indian and Pacific Oceans. Production could barely keep pace with demand for the aircraft. By 1943, the Castle

Bromwich factory was operating twenty-four hours a day with a peak workforce of no fewer than 15,854. An extraordinary mix of people from all walks of life were now involved in the Spitfire's construction. In March 2006, a *Daily Telegraph* obituary of the eccentric Scottish humorist, poet and songwriter Ivor Cutler caught my eye: 'After working as an apprentice fitter for Rolls-Royce helping to make Spitfires,' it read, 'he joined the RAF in 1942.' Even a man best known in later years for nonsense poems and for his role as Buster Bloodvessel, manic driver of the blue-and-yellow coach in the Beatles' psychedelic film *Magical Mystery Tour* (1968), was a part of the extraordinary international effort to build and fly Spitfires. And to defeat Hitler, Mussolini and Hirohito.

Up and down the British Isles there were public offerings of aluminium pots and pans to help build Spitfires. Some two thousand organizations had Spitfires named after them, having each raised £5,000, mostly in 'tanners', or sixpences, towards the cost of their manufacture. Spitfire pilots took to the air in machines with names that ranged from the inspired to the perhaps slightly less successful – from 'Dog Fighter (Kennel Club)' to 'The National Federation of Hosiery Manufacturers'. One Spitfire sported the famous red and blue bull's eye motif of the London Passenger Transport Board. This made sense; Spitfires played a critical role in the defence of London, and what was, at the time, the finest integrated public transport system in the world had been one of the very things, along with freedom, decency and Poland, that had been well worth fighting for. London Underground stations sheltered Londoners during the Blitz. Indeed, the LPTB's chief executive Frank Pick wrote a fine essay, 'Paths to Peace' (1941), outlining the sort of Britain everyone was, or ought to be, fighting to preserve and improve.

Spitfire pilots themselves, by the middle of the war, were drawn from all over the world. At the Science Museum exhibition in 2005 I looked at a photograph of a beturbaned young Sikh pilot, Squadron Leader Mahinder Singh Pujii. A qualified pilot working for Shell Oil in India, he had volunteered to join the RAF as early as August 1940 and flew Spitfire Mk Vs in operational sorties across London, as well as Europe. I got to shake his hand at the exhibition devoted to the Spitfire curated by Andrew Nahum. Another photograph depicted dashing young Sergeant, later Flying Officer, James Joseph Hyde, a black West Indian, playing with his squadron's mascot, a fluffy dog called Dingo, wagging his tail on the wing of a Spitfire. Hyde was shot down and killed on

Spitfire pilot Flight Sergeant James Hyde, from Trinidad, in December 1943.

25 September 1944. Here also was Sergeant Vincent Bunting, another black West Indian, from Kingston, Jamaica, in conversation with the great Spitfire ace 'Sailor' Malan at Biggin Hill.

Meanwhile, there were Free French Spitfire squadrons in England, New Zealanders and Indians flying Spitfires over Calcutta, Australians flying Spitfires against the Japanese from Darwin, just as there were Soviet Air Force or VVS pilots flying Spitfires against Bf 109s and Fw 190s west of the Urals, and Germans infamously using captured Spitfires to strafe towns on the east coast of England. Americans flew Spitfires too, and in time the British fighter even began to acquire something of the look of the powerful new North American P-51D Mustang long-range fighter. Later versions of the Mustang were, of course, powered by an American-built version of the Merlin, an engine that, in turn, had its mechanical roots in the race-proved Curtiss D-12 of 1921.

If the Spitfire became, somehow, a little Yankee Doodle in the latter part of the war, this was not surprising. By 1943, Britain and the United States were working closely together on plans for the invasion of Nazi-occupied Europe, while from that year on, Spitfires in South-East Asia were flying alongside American Army, Navy and Marine Corps fighters in the war against Japan. Meanwhile, American soldiers and airmen were oversexed, overpaid and over here. They brought some of their particular know-how, muscle and braggadocio to Britain, along with the kind of hip-twisting music and dance, smartly scripted movies and Hollywood-style lingo that RAF pilots, however stiff-lipped their background, appeared to have lapped up like hungry, and increasingly cool, cats.

The movies, of course, strongly influenced many young men dreaming of becoming fighter pilots in the 1930s. Wilfrid Duncan

Smith says that he saw *Dawn Patrol* four times. This was the 1938 remake, directed by Edmund Golding, of a film the Hollywood giant, D. W. Griffith, had made eight years before, starring Douglas Fairbanks Jr. The latest version that so mesmerized young Duncan Smith featured the dashing Errol Flynn and debonair David Niven as First World War Royal Flying Corps pilots fighting both the will of their anguished CO, played wonderfully well by Basil Rathbone, and Huns in the sun over the mud of the Somme. It was good, rattling machine-gun stuff. Every aspiring RAF pilot wanted to be a bit like Flynn or Niven in *Dawn Patrol*. There were, rather interestingly, no women in the film. They would, I suppose, have been a diversion too far.

In reality, Supermarine had been busy right through the Battle of Britain, developing more powerful versions of its now famous fighter. No one, least of all those who flew her in action, doubted the flying abilities of the Spitfire, but she needed to pack a greater punch than she had done in the summer of 1940. The Mk IV Spitfire, scheduled to fly in August 1941, was to have been powered by the 37-litre Griffon engine developed from the Schneider Trophy-winning Rolls-Royce R-Type. In theory, the Griffon would raise the Spit's top speed to 420 mph and allow it to climb to 15,000 feet in just four and a half minutes. Excited by the prospect, the RAF requested that the Mk IV's armament should comprise either six 20-mm cannon, or two 20-mm cannon and eight Brownings, or even a dozen Brownings. Not surprisingly, this quantum leap in the design, performance and firepower of the Spitfire was a little over-ambitious. Although the first Mk IV flew on 27 November 1941, Castle Bromwich was by then both mass-producing the Mk V, the natural replacement for the Mk I and II, and converting older aircraft to the new specification. Alex

Henshaw, one of the Spitfire's chief test pilots, was busy testing up to twenty new aircraft a day at Castle Bromwich.

The Mk V was the most numerous of the many Spitfire marks. No fewer than 6,787 were built. It had been intended as a stop-gap between the Mk I and II and the new Griffon-powered Mk IV. In the event, the arrival of the latest Messerschmitt Bf 109F, an altogether more potent machine than the 109E that had been such a familiar sight over South-East England in 1940, encouraged the RAF, Supermarine and Rolls-Royce to speed ahead with an improved Merlin-powered design. The Griffon could wait. At above 25,000 feet, the Bf 109F could easily outperform early Spitfires. The Mk V retained the purity of outline and the superb handling characteristics of the Mk I, yet, with the 45 and 46 models of the Merlin now producing 1,230 hp, it was easily a match for the latest version of its old foe. Its top speed was 369 mph, and it could climb to 35,000 feet in fifteen minutes. Some Mk Vs had their wing tips clipped by more than two feet; this detracted from their looks but was meant to improve their low-level handling, an important consideration in the new world of flak-defying Rhubarbs and sitting-duck Circuses. However, such machines were not popular, especially as the all-important climbing ability of the aircraft was impaired.

The Spitfire's limited fuel capacity, not so much of a worry in the Battle of Britain when sorties tended to be dizzily brief affairs, proved to be much more of a handicap now that the fighter was asked to fly extended missions. At its optimum cruising speed of 281 mph at 10,000 feet, with the engine set at 2,650 rpm, and the supercharger boosted to +2 lbs pressure – a pressure that enabled the engine to produce great power at high altitudes where the air it needed to make petrol burn efficiently is thinner and so less potent – a Mk V knocked back thirty-five gallons of 100-octane petrol an hour. The tank held eighty-seven gallons. You can do the maths for yourself. At the maximum continuous cruise of 331 mph, at 2,650 rpm and +6 lbs boost, a Mk V guzzled seventy gallons an hour. In combat, with the throttle pushed full forward, the engine at its 3,000-rpm red-line and at +16 lbs maximum boost, a full tank would be emptied in a little over thirty minutes. In action, of course, there was no alternative. An Air Ministry Air Tactics Department manual for Mk V pilots issued in August 1942 advised, after much crisp and useful technical information, 'when in the vicinity of Huns, fly maximum everything and in good time'. American business-speak, happily, had yet to invade Britain.

Only the new, unarmed photo-reconnaissance Spitfires had anything like a long range: devoid of guns, the generous leading edges of their wings could be used as fuel tanks, and extra fuel tanks were added in the fuselage behind the pilot, and in drop tanks below. Only then was it a piece of cake to fly to Germany and back. A Mk V, no matter how good a fighter, could only spend a brief while flying Rhubarbs over France before its pilot nosed back to base, for debriefing, refuelling and beer.

After clipping a number of Mk V wings to achieve improved low-level handling, Joe Smith's team also busied themselves with high flight. The Mk VI Spitfire of 1941 had long wings with pointed rather than gracefully rounded tips and, for the first time, a pressurized cabin: it was intended to combat the perceived threat of high-flying German bombers and reconnaissance aircraft. But Hitler's invasion of the Soviet Union in June 1941 saw the Luftwaffe concentrating its maximum effort on Operation Barbarossa, and during this slight lull RAF squadrons were re-equipped with

Mk Vs as soon as this was possible. Meanwhile, the RAF kept up its high rate of missions over France partly in a bid to draw at least some of the Luftwaffe's fighters away from the Russian front. It proved a costly tactic, both in terms of aircraft destroyed and pilots lost. Douglas Bader was forced to bail out over enemy territory on one of these missions on 9 August when his Spitfire Mk V collided with a Bf 109F. For the tin-legged ace, the war was over. In fact, over 200 RAF fighter pilots were lost in June, July and August 1941. It was simply too much to bear: in November, Churchill ordered the temporary suspension of Rhubarbs.

In March 1941, the Spitfire had received a significant boost in terms of its aerobatic and thus its fighting ability. It was known, among grateful, if cocky pilots, as 'Miss Shilling's Orifice'. The 'orifice' in question was a hole the size of an old threepenny bit punched through a metal diaphragm placed across the float chambers of the Merlin's SU carburettors. This simple device solved the infamous problem of the Spitfire and the negative-g manoeuvre. Previously, when the Spitfire was thrust into sudden dives, the carburettors would suffer fuel loss, causing the engine to cut out. Although not dangerous – the Merlin would always come on song again in a matter of moments – this had proved to be a curse for many Battle of Britain pilots. Breaking off to dive after a Bf 109 they felt confident was in the bag, they would find their engine spluttering as they tried to pounce on their target – unless, that is, they performed a half-roll, or even turned the aircraft on its back to restore the flow of fuel. All this took precious seconds as well as being unnecessarily uncomfortable. With its fuel-injected motor, a Messerschmitt could be nosed precipitously into the steepest, full-throttle dive without the slightest hiccup. Rolls-Royce persisted with its use of carburettors on the basis that the greater density of the fuel-air mixture inside a carburettor, compared to that of fuel-injection systems, gave its engine an advantage in power. This was entirely consistent with what W. O. Bentley, a one-time locomotive apprentice with the Great Northern Railway, liked to call the 'sheer bloody thump' of the big, carb-fuelled engines that helped 'Babe' Barnato outgun fancy little Continental racers at Le Mans in the late 1920s.

Miss Beatrice 'Tilly' Shilling, a thirty-two-year-old scientist at the Royal Aircraft Establishment, Farnborough, as well as a keen racing motorcyclist and, in the words of one of her colleagues, a 'flaming pathfinder of women's lib', was the heroine of the moment. The Shilling solution was not perfect, but it helped enormously until Rolls-Royce developed an anti-g version of the SU carburettor in 1942. Further improvements, with various forms of ingenious hybrid fuel-flow systems, were made through-out the long life, and prodigious production run, of the Merlin. Even with this modification, however, the Mk V was about to be trounced by a formidable new opponent, the Focke-Wulf Fw 190, a BMW radial-engined fighter designed by Kurt Tank. Although in service from the autumn of 1941, this fast-rolling, lethal German fighter was only encountered in strength at the beginning of 1942. By now Fighter Command had sixty squadrons of Spitfires, flown by a bewildering array of foreign nationals as well as British-born pilots. Communication in the air between these polyglot flyers could sometimes be limited. This was not exactly helpful when the Focke-Wulf pounced. By April, the Fw 190 was master, mistress and all Prussian princes of the skies above France; in that month alone, the RAF lost fifty-nine Spitfires. Something needed to be done, and quickly.

Helpfully, an Fw 190, a little lost, landed at RAF Pembrey Sands on the South Wales coast. It was pitted against a Mk V; the Spitfire turned faster – that wing again – but was otherwise outclassed in every way. This led to the extraordinarily rapid development of the Mk IX, a vamped-up Mk V equipped with a potent two-speed, two-stage supercharged Merlin 60 series engine, and a four-bladed prop. The Mk IX proved to be 40 mph faster than the Mk V and was quicker than the Fw 190 in almost every way, even at low level, where the German fighter excelled. Delivery to RAF squadrons began with 64 Squadron, Hornchurch, in June 1942. Supermarine had intended the Mk VIII to answer the threat posed by the Fw 190, but the type's development was slower than expected and so priority was given to the Mk IX.

The work on the new superchargers had been carried out at Rolls-Royce by Stanley Hooker, a mathematician by training. Hooker persisted in his aim of squeezing ever more power from the Merlin. In late 1944, he had one of the engines pumping out an heroic 2,640 hp for a full fifteen minutes. Although this was a test-bed engine and not expected to run in service, Hooker's team was eventually able to extract a reliable maximum of 2,030 hp from the Merlin, more than twice the power of the engine that had driven K5054 into the air above Eastleigh in 1936. Imagine if, in 1961, Jaguar had offered an E-Type for sale with 530 bhp on tap.

If the Mk IX was considerably faster in every respect than the Mk V, it was less sweet to fly. This was nothing to do with the engine or airframe as such, but because of a new fuel tank added behind the pilot. The extra power meant that with just the regular 87-gallon tank ahead of the pilot, the Mk IX's range would have been nugatory. Pilots found that the tank upset the aircraft's longitudinal stability; they had to work hard to keep the Mk IX in straight and level flight until at least half of the rear tank was emptied. Only then did the aircraft come into its own and feel like a thoroughbred Spitfire should. Pilots were recommended not to engage in combat until they had used up the fuel in the rear tank. While this would have been an absurd order during the Battle of Britain – Spitfires were expected to climb straight up into battle when Dowding's Ops Rooms happened to be caught off guard – the Mk IX operated in a completely different theatre of war. Once in action, though, the Mk IX was a magnificent fighter. Johnnie Johnson, the RAF's top-scoring ace, made many of his thirty-eight kills with the guns of EN398; naturally, he thought the Mk IX the best Spitfire of all.

The Mk IX was first pressed into service, alongside the Mk V, for Operation Jubilee, a disastrous, small-scale precursor to D-Day carried out by 6,000 Canadian troops put ashore at Dieppe on 19 August 1942. Of the 106 allied aircraft lost that day, eighty-eight were fighters and most of them Spitfires. At the end of September, the American Eagle Spitfire squadrons became a part of the USAAF. Mk IXs were now used to escort B-17 Flying Fortresses on bombing raids, another role for which they were clearly unsuited. The Mk IX excelled at high flight, and so much so that its performance now outstripped that of its pilots. It could fly happily at 43,000 feet, beyond the reach of existing German fighters; this is higher than the altitude at which Boeing 747s, 777s and even the latest generation of A380 Airbuses fly across the Atlantic. Without pressurized cockpits, even the fittest pilot could only remain at such an Olympian height for five, or at best, ten minutes. And if pilots swept down too quickly from such altitudes, they would be in very real danger of suffering what divers, coming up to the surface too quickly, know as 'the bends': agonizingly painful, and sometimes even fatal. Despite this, in Malta in April 1942, a Spitfire Mk VB was stripped of its armour and equipped with just a pair of 0.5-inch machine-guns for high-altitude sorties. With its Merlin tweaked for added power and a four-bladed prop in place of the usual three-bladed design, the fighter climbed to 42,000 feet and intercepted and destroyed one of the previously unassailable Junkers Ju 86P reconnaissance aircraft. Subsequently, on 12 September 1942, another modified Spitfire, this time a Mk IX, met a Ju 86R at 43,500 feet over Southampton in what was to prove the highest recorded combat of the war.

By the summer of 1942, Malta had been under siege for more than two years. Basking in the Mediterranean just below Sicily, the island remained a thorn in the side of the Axis. They wanted it as an island aircraft carrier for the Regia Aeronautica and the Luftwaffe and as a transit camp for troop movements between Europe and North Africa, where Rommel's Afrika Korps and Italian forces were fighting the British Eighth Army. The British and the Americans, who had entered the war after the Japanese attack on Pearl Harbor on 7 December 1941, were just as determined to keep Malta for themselves: it lay across the enemy's most direct lines of supply and would serve as a springboard for any invasion of Sicily, and thus Italy.

Malta had stoically borne the brunt of horrific air raids, and such was the courage shown by its inhabitants that George VI was to award the island the George Cross. It had initially been protected by a paltry number of Gloster Gladiators and later by Hurricanes. Then the cavalry arrived, in the shape of the Spitfire. This was the Spitfire's first posting abroad. It proved not just to be successful, but a turning point in the destiny of Mitchell's astounding design. On 7 March 1942, fifteen Mk Vs carrying ninety-gallon fuel tanks under their slim bellies took off from the deck of the carrier HMS *Eagle* off the coast of Algeria on a hazardous 600-mile flight to Malta. Nine more arrived, the same way, on the 21st, and a further seven on the 29th. Axis bombers more than redoubled their attacks on Malta. In March and April 1942 alone, it is believed that more bombs fell on Malta than on London throughout the Blitz. Yet still the Spitfires continued to come, flying from the *Eagle*, the much larger American carrier USS *Wasp* and the *Furious*. The carriers out at sea, though, were thought to be vulnerable to attack from the Luftwaffe and so it was decided to fly Spitfires, now equipped with bulky 170-gallon drop tanks, from Gibraltar itself the 1,100 miles to Malta. With the big fuel tanks slowing the aircraft, this meant a flight time of more than five hours.

In July, Air Vice Marshal Park arrived, newly appointed head of the island's air defence. The enemy, principally the Luftwaffe's Luftflotte 2 recently returned from the Russian front, was led by Park's old Battle of Britain adversary, Field Marshal Kesselring. Eventually Park had twenty Spitfire squadrons under his command, and quite a number of his senior pilots – for example, Brian Kingcombe, who went on to make sofas in the Cotswolds after the war, and took out advertising in the *Architectural Review* while I was assistant editor there in the 1980s – were Battle of Britain veterans.

In fact, Park reorganized fighter tactics very much along the lines he had adopted in the summer of 1940. This paid off. Within a remarkably short spell, the RAF's Spitfires, with many of the Mk Vs now equipped to carry a pair of 250-lb bombs attached beneath their wings, turned from defender to aggressor. The Spitfires were now used as makeshift dive-bombers, raiding Sicilian fortifications and air bases, and releasing their bombs at 7,000 feet as they dived at an optimum angle of 60 degrees. Not exactly Stukas, but then a Ju 87 could never have launched a ground attack and then turned to climb and tussle, on at least equal terms, with Fw 190s, Bf 109s and the Regia Aeronautica's two best fighters, the Daimler-Benz-powered Macchi MC 202 and 205.

Malta also provided an opportunity for Spitfire pilots to engage in Battle of Britain-style dogfights at which, of course, their aircraft excelled. George 'Buzz' Beurling, a twenty-two-year-old Canadian, who had tried to fight with the Chinese against the Japanese, the Finns against the Russians, and with the RCAF, before being accepted by the RAF as a sergeant pilot in 1942, was the top-scoring ace in the fight for, and from, Malta. His score, which he later raised to thirty-two, was twenty-seven. Shot down four times over Malta, Beurling is said to have owed his spectacular success to a remarkably good eye and violent flying. If jumped from behind, he would pull back on the stick of his Mk VC Spitfire so hard that the aircraft would enter a violent stall, flick over and spin. This was a hard, sudden and very dangerous act for the enemy fighter on his tail to follow. Or Beurling would ram both ailerons and rudder into a sudden and violent turn, causing his Spitfire to flip over and drop like a stone. Only a very experienced or crazy pilot would pull such stunts more than once or twice. Beurling made them a matter of habit. He knew that the Spitfire could be nursed out of such self-induced trouble and get him home safely. He survived the war but was one of a number of former Spitfire pilots drawn to fly and fight again in the Israeli War of Independence. In May 1948 the light transport aircraft he was ferrying to Israel crashed after taking off from Rome, killing Canada's and Malta's top-scoring ace.

Air Vice Marshal Sir Keith Park, previously the commander of 11 Group in the Battle of Britain, preparing to fly his Spitfire on Malta in September 1942.

Most of the pilots thought conditions on Malta were lousy, and the food was very bad. But they liked the girls and the beaches, and the lucky ones hung out drinking beer, pink gin and wine, at Charlie's Bar and the Chocolate King. Brian Kingcombe had got hold of a yacht, and so there was sailing for the very few from St Paul's Bay in between raids and sorties from the island's runway at Luqa. This was not an experience shared by everyone involved with Spitfires on Malta, GC. Leading Aircraftsman George Howes recalled how rib-revealing rationing had hit hard by the height of the summer. 'The main meal of the day, supper, would usually be a thin slice of bread with some bully beef and a small portion of potatoes with, sometimes, if we were lucky, some dried vegetables, but seldom enough to allay one's hunger. At Safi village just off the airfield an old woman ran a black-market eating house. We had to pay five shillings for a rather foul pancake made out of flour and water, fried in Spitfire hydraulic oil which we had to bring ourselves; and we had to queue for the privilege.'

However hungry, or hung over, Spitfire pilots and their ground crews fought hard under Park's inspired direction, working closely now with their American colleagues, who undertook most of the heavy-duty bombing. With the surrender of Axis forces in North Africa in May 1943, large numbers of aircraft previously tied down in the fight there now flew in to Luqa. Within a year of the arrival of those first Spitfire Mk Vs from the deck of HMS *Eagle*, the Allies had built up a combined air force of some 4,000 aircraft on Malta. Park estimated that, between them, the Germans and Italians could field, at the very most, 2,000 aircraft. Sicily fell to the Allies on 17 August 1943 after thirty-eight days of fierce fighting across the island, during which Spitfires were fully employed sweeping the skies of enemy fighters. When Sicily fell, so did Mussolini, convinced all those years ago that his Savoia and Macchi seaplanes would bring the Schneider Trophy home to Rome. He was defeated, with a little help from Supermarine, both then and now again in 1943. The Spitfire's first away assignment had been a great success.

But, if Spitfire pilots revelled in the part they had played over Malta and Sicily, and knew that in Air Vice Marshal Park they were led by a commander utterly committed to them, then their German counterparts were not so fortunate. A captured Luftwaffe Order of the Day during the invasion of Sicily read churlishly: 'Together with the fighter pilots in France, Norway and Russia, I can only regard you with contempt. If an immediate improvement is not forthcoming, flying personnel from the Kommodore downwards must expect to be reduced to the ranks and transferred to the Eastern Front to serve on the ground. Signed, Reichsmarshal Hermann Goering.'

Henceforth, Spitfire squadrons were to support the Allied armies as they battled their bloody way north through Italy. Initially they would be based alongside the ancient Greek temples on the coast at Paestum, and take part in the nightmare assault on Monte Cassino. Pilots, although enjoying when they could the sensual joys of local life, found, after Italy's surrender in September 1943, that the Germans seemed to be fighting harder than ever, and brutally so, massacring civilians as they retreated to Florence. But men such as Wilfrid Duncan Smith were to become hardened. Later, on a strafing raid through southern France in the autumn of 1944, he opened up on what transpired to be a Red Cross ambulance. In the evening he drove out to the spot and found a makeshift communal grave beside the burned-out ambulance, marked by a cross bearing the names of the fifteen wounded German soldiers he had killed early that morning. 'The ambulance incident was unfortunate, but unavoidable,' Duncan Smith was to write. 'I remembered a morning in England, during the summer of 1942, when I saw an Fw 190 fighter-bomber strafe the main shopping area of Folkestone, which at the time was full of women; I couldn't do anything about it because I was unable to catch him. Looking at the names on the cross, I reckoned it was a just retribution.'

The invasion of Sicily, and the landings at Salerno on mainland Italy, had been achieved with the help of carrier-based Seafires flying alongside the Maltese Spitfires. The Seafire, the naval version of the Spitfire, first saw action on 8 November 1942 during Operation Torch, the Allied invasion of Morocco and Algeria, when a Mk IB of 801 Squadron, flown from the deck of HMS *Furious*, shot down a French Dewoitine D 520. This Hispano-Suiza-powered machine was probably the best of the French fighters – production had even recommenced, with German blessing, in Vichy France – but it was easily outclassed by the Seafire. Interestingly, an earlier model of the Dewoitine had been fitted with a Rolls-Royce Merlin. But that was in 1939, before the Battle of France.

The Seafire was a far from ideal naval fighter, and its narrow undercarriage alone should have disqualified it from carrier operations. Its performance in the air, though, impressed the Royal Navy as it did everyone else, friend and foe alike. Equipped with an arrestor hook, attachments for catapult launches and, in later variants, folding wings, the Spitfire took to an unlikely life on the ocean wave. More Seafires, however, were put out of action by crash-landing on the decks of carriers than by enemy action. Yet they remained superb interceptors, and were improved over the years to such an extent that the last of the line, the magnificent

Mk 47, which, with its 2,300-hp engine and twin, contra-rotating propellers, weighed twice as much as a Mk I Spitfire, flew in combat during the jet-age Korean War and remained in service with the Royal Navy Volunteer Reserve (RNVR) until 1954.

Although Supermarine had approached the Admiralty as early as 1938 with plans for a custom-designed seagoing Spitfire, these were rejected in favour of the slower and less agile two-seater Fairey Fulmar. The Fulmar boasted a Merlin engine and eight Browning .303s but its top speed was just 266 mph and it had little of the Spitfire's ability to climb, duck or dive. By late 1941, the Navy was well aware that it needed a fighter that could take on not just German Bf 109s but also the new threat posed by the Japanese Imperial Navy's Mitsubishi A6M2 Zero fighters. Even then, the first Seafires, which went into service on board HMS *Illustrious* on 10 February 1942, were really only slightly modified Spitfire Mk Vs. The Admiralty had to wait until November 1943 for delivery of the Seafire Mk III, a machine with folding wings that could be stored below deck. The first Griffon-powered Seafire, the Mk XV, arrived in May 1945. By the war's end that August, there were twelve frontline Seafire squadrons operating from six Royal Navy carriers. One of their final duties – as the Japanese made the painful discovery that the war, in the memorable words of Emperor Hirohito, 'had developed not necessarily to Japan's advantage' – was to defend Allied warships from attacks by kamikaze suicide planes. This was a very long way indeed from dogfighting Bf 109s over the English Channel.

A Spitfire floatplane, recalling the glorious days of the Schneider Trophy, had also been developed as early as 1940 when a Mk I was converted as a fighter with the potential to fight from fjords during the German invasion of Norway. Like the campaign it was prepared for, but never flown in, R6722 was not exactly a success. It was dubbed the 'Narvik Nightmare'. The idea was revived at the beginning of the war in the Pacific against Japan. Given the sheer number of islands this war was conducted on, over and across, and the long distances over sea involved, a floatplane that could fight its way as it hopped from island to island made a certain sense. Folland Aircraft was charged with the conversion of W3760, a Mk VB, and with generally good handling and a top speed of 324 mph the result was considered a success. The first three floatplanes were shipped not to the Pacific, but to Egypt, in October 1943. They were to be flown from unoccupied Greek islands in the Dodecanese against transport planes supplying German-held islands. The Germans, however, quickly overran the entire area, scuppering the floatplane plan. In 1944, one more floatplane was made, converted from a Mk IX. This fine machine had a top speed of 377 mph, but found little to do. Imagine owning her for the holiday trips of a lifetime today.

In early 1943, Spitfires finally made it to the other end of the world. Mk Vs were sent down under to equip 54 Squadron, Darwin. The capital of Australia's Northern Territory had been exposed to Japanese bombing raids. It needed Spitfires. The squadron's first kill was made on 6 February, when Flight Lieutenant Tony Foster, one of the Few and now back home, shot down a high-flying Mitsubishi Ki-46 Dinah reconnaissance plane. The squadron was later equipped with much-loved Mk VIIIs, four-bladed machines with special air filters for tropical service, and powered by twin-supercharger Merlins providing up to 1,710 hp. Spitfires had also gone to the aid of 'Uncle Joe' Stalin. In November 1941, the RAF had sent three PR Mk IV Spitfires to Vaenga in northern Russia to keep an eye on the movement of German warships. The Soviet VVS had been suitably impressed. The following May, 143 Mk VBs were sent to Russia, and between then and the fall of Berlin some 1,200 Mk IXs followed.

Meanwhile, the first Griffon-powered Spitfires, with never less than 1,700 hp under their big noses, made their debut in squadron service in early 1943. They were designated Mk XII and had been developed from the largely experimental Mk IV first flown in late 1941. The main difference between the Griffon and the Merlin, aside from a big increase in cubic capacity and sheer power, was the way in which the Griffon's engine turned in the opposite direction to a Merlin's. Take-off had always been tricky for Spitfire pilots, just as it was for the pilots of all propeller-driven aircraft. The turning, or torque effect, of the propeller causes an aircraft to pull strongly away from the straight-ahead position as it gathers speed down the runway. The pilot controls this with his feet on the rudder; the flow of air directed across the rudder counterbalances the aircraft's natural desire, driven by the direction in which its engine spins, to chase its own tail. So the pilots of Griffon-powered Spitfires had to relearn what for most had become second nature – and if they ever did have a momentary lapse and flick the rudder the wrong way, they would find the aircraft trying to take off, at best, sideways.

The Griffon's engine did not turn in the opposite direction to the Merlin's as a result of some bizarre desire on the part of Rolls-Royce's engineers to keep battle-fatigued fighter pilots on their toes. No, it was because a decision had been made by the Society of British Aircraft Constructors to establish the common workings of a 'universal power plant'. The engines of Bristol, Napier and Armstrong-Siddeley all turned in the opposite direction to those of Rolls-Royce. Outnumbered three to one, Rolls-Royce agreed to follow suit.

While the captured Fw 190 was being put through its paces at Farnborough in June 1942, the RAF organized an air race between the German fighter and the thundering new Hawker Typhoon. Hawker was trumpeting the immensely powerful, if nose-heavy, Typhoon as the fighter of the future. Supermarine was asked to act as a referee. It sent Jeffrey Quill in DP845, one of the first two Mk IVs. The Spitfire was meant to pace the two faster fighters, but as the Typhoon and Fw 190 raced towards the finishing line, Quill, following sedately behind them, unleashed the full might of the Griffon and shot ahead to win the 'race'. By the time it was married to the Mk XII airframe, the Griffon was good for 2,035 hp. This gave the Mk XII superb performance at low levels and, competing directly with the Typhoon, it soon proved an Fw 190 killer. What it did not have was the easy high-altitude performance of the Mk IX, nor could it be rolled so easily. In fact, the Mk IX did not roll as easily as the balletic Mk V. But this was par for the course. The Mk V did not roll so well as the Mk I, and the Mk I was just that little bit less nimble than K5054. In putting on weight, the Spitfire was to lose something of its aerobatic grace. As it was, the Mk IX offered perhaps the best compromise between speed, power, punch and agility, and continued in production at Castle Bromwich until the end of the war. The Mk XII was also, although undeniably impressive, less graceful than the svelte Mk IX. The cylinder heads of the chunky Griffon erupted in streamlined blisters along either side of the aircraft's nose, and a third blister encased the magnetos.

Only one hundred Mk XIIs were built as it was a bit of a beast to fly. Supermarine's quick-thinking solution was to mate the fuselage of the Mk VIII Spitfire with the Griffon. This resulted in the Mk XIV, of which 957 were built. The Mk XIV performed well and was much easier to fly, for a number of reasons. One of these was a longer throttle travel. Pilots with experience of the Mk XII discovered, not to their advantage, that even a slight push forwards on the throttle prompted a massive surge of power from the flame-throwing Griffon. But a newly developed five-blade Rotol propeller made optimum use of all that spinning, growling energy, and clipped wings decreased the strain on the fuselage. The daunting Mk XIV finally went into service with 610 (County of Chester) Squadron in the spring of 1944. Its guns packed three times the punch of those of a Mk I and its top speed was 450 mph at 26,000 feet. It could climb at 4,580 feet per minute, meaning that within eight seconds it would have put the height of the British Telecom Tower between it and a Mk IX flying flat out behind and below it. It went into action not so much against late-model Bf 109s and Fw 190s as, very effectively, against the V1 flying bomb, of which it destroyed at least 300, saving the lives of thousands of Londoners in the last eighteen months of the war. And it was a burly Mk XIV that became the first Allied aircraft to shoot down one of the Luftwaffe's Messerschmitt Me 262 jet fighters.

Later Mk XIVs were equipped with teardrop canopies which gave Spitfire pilots unobstructed, all-round vision for the first time. Johnnie Johnson said that the Mk XIV was a fine machine, but no longer a Spitfire. It was certainly beginning to resemble the P-51D Mustang, if not quite the truly enormous Republic P-47 Thunderbolt, the 2,800-hp US fighter piloted in the late stages of the war by, among others, the survivors of the Spitfire Eagle squadrons. The wing tip of the P-47 was higher than the cockpit canopy of a Mk IX Spitfire.

That the Spitfire was a fast aircraft no one could deny. But just how fast? From May 1943, the Royal Aircraft Establishment began a lengthy series of high-speed test dives to investigate the handling of aircraft approaching the sound barrier. On 27 April 1944, a Mk XI, a reconnaissance version of the ubiquitous Mk IX, flown by Flight Lieutenant 'Marty' Martindale, reached the unprecedented speed of 606 mph in a 45-degree dive; this was a little under Mach 0.9. The Spitfire was on its way to breaking the sound barrier. But before it could do so, the propeller's constant-speed unit gave up the ghost. Engine and airscrew turned faster and faster until both broke up. Cool as a cucumber, Martindale glided the Spitfire for twenty miles, losing height in a controlled manner, and brought the record-breaking EN409 to land safely at Farnborough.

There was one further claim. In 1951, a PR XIX, the reconnaissance version of the Griffon-powered Mk XIV, on meteorological duties with 81 Squadron, Hong Kong, climbed to no less than 51,550 feet, the world record for a piston-engined aircraft. This was as close to the sun as a Spitfire was going to get before being burned and, like Icarus, falling to earth. Flight Lieutenant Ted Powles was just able to maintain flight above the stall at that extraordinary height when, suddenly, a warning light flashed on. Cabin pressure was falling. Powles needed to lose height, and quickly. But not so fast that he found himself unable to pull out of the ensuing dive, which is what happened. Because of the reversal of the ailerons at this immense speed, the aircraft only came out of the dive, at somewhere below 3,000 feet, when Powles pushed the stick forwards, the very opposite of what his intuition, let alone his training, would have been telling him. His air speed indicator had registered 690 mph, or 0.94 Mach, at 15,000 feet. The aircraft landed safely and quite undamaged.

While there is no questioning the altitude record set that day, the maximum speed was to remain unconfirmed as the relevant instruments proved to be faulty. Whatever the truth, the Spitfire, fifteen years on from the first flight of K5054 over Eastleigh, was flying somewhere, thousands of miles from home, at an extraordinary rate for a piston-engined aircraft dating back to 1936. In this sense, the Spitfire was a junction box between early flight and the jet age, and one of the key stepping stones to successful supersonic flight in the 1950s. 'That any operational aircraft off the production line,' wrote Jeffrey Quill, 'cannon sprouting from its wings, and warts and all, could readily be controlled at this speed [Powles's alleged 690 mph] when the early jet aircraft such as Meteors, Vampires, [Lockheed] P-80s etc could not, was certainly extraordinary.' Again, it was the wing profile that made all the difference between the Spitfire and its less aerodynamic contemporaries. As Sir Morien Morgan, the distinguished Welsh aerodynamicist, has said: 'Considering that he could have had little knowledge of Mach effects, Mitchell's decision to use such a thin wing was not only bold, but inspired. We now know that it was a close-run thing: had he made the wing a little thinner it would probably have been too weak, and aileron reversal would have been encountered lower down the speed scale. And, if that had happened, the Spitfire would have been just one more of those aircraft that did not quite make the grade.' Sir Morien, if anyone, would have known: between 1948 and 1959, he directed the programme of research into the feasibility of a supersonic passenger aircraft that led to Concorde.

It was the Spitfire's speed and agility that kept it ahead of the game right to the end of the war. On 7 March 1945, Flight Lieutenant Raby of 542 Squadron was flying a PR XI on a reconnaissance mission to photograph a power station and oil depot south of Leipzig, and to record the effects of a Bomber Command raid two nights before on Chemnitz. Raby's mission had seemed like a piece of applestrudel – until Chemnitz. Climbing up from the airfield at a rate of 10,000 feet per minute was a pair of Me 163 rocket-powered interceptors. These, though, proved to be too fast in a straight line, and not quick enough in the turn. Twisting and turning at diving speeds of 500 mph, Raby not only saw off his attackers but completed his mission before heading for home.

During the later stages of the Second World War, however, it was reliability in all weathers and low-level performance that mattered more than sheer speed. The Spitfire was in demand across the Indian subcontinent and South-East Asia, although it was slow to arrive in anything like adequate numbers. This was understandable given the demands already being made on the aircraft, and the factories making it, in Europe. The air defence of British imperial territory in Singapore, Malaya and Burma was, at the outset of the war with Japan, the responsibility of just five day-fighter squadrons, operated by the RAF, the RAAF and the RNZAF, flying the Brewster Buffalo, a slow, chunky American fighter. They were backed up by a single night-fighter squadron equipped with Bristol Blenheims. In eastern India, a single squadron of obsolete and under-armed Curtiss P-36A Mohawks stood ready in the defence of the Raj. There was no equivalent of Air Chief Marshal Dowding in India or South-East Asia, no early warning system worth mentioning, and, it must be said, no real understanding, much less appreciation, of the enemy. When the

Japanese overran Singapore and then Burma in 1942, their success came as an almighty shock.

With their troops massed on the north Burmese border, the Japanese could contemplate the invasion of India and the overthrow of the Raj. But Operation O-GU was not a particularly easy proposition. The only real land route lay up and across the densely tropical Naga Hills to the garrison town of Kohima, where Charles Pawsey, district governor of Nagaland, lived in a charming bungalow with tennis courts and lovingly tended gardens. From there it was, theoretically at least, and out of the monsoon season, a comfortable march down through the tea plantations of Assam and on to teeming Calcutta. Led by Lieutenant General Renya Mutaguchi, the Japanese Fifteenth Army finally began its march through the jungle on 4 April 1944. The Japanese scythed their way through to Kohima on 6 April. The fiercest fighting there, the Battle of the Tennis Courts, was around Pawsey's bungalow. It was no laughing matter. By 17 April, it looked as if Kohima would fall and the Japanese would come pouring down the hillsides into Assam, putting the decadent British and their Empire to flight.

Flight, though, is what made all the difference. My father did talk a little about Kohima. Born the son of an Indian Army general in Lahore, baptized in St Paul's Cathedral, Calcutta, and educated there at the grand, white stucco, neo-classical La Martinère school, he always loved India and, in particular, the Himalayas. Although he was more often than not to be found at the races in Calcutta, he particularly liked Nagaland, where the eastern tail of the mountains sloped down into the jungles of Burma. He loved these tropical hills, the spectacular flowers that adorned them in spring, and the extraordinary Naga tribespeople themselves. Headhunters then, these tartan-clad warriors stood by the British as the Japanese invaded their hills. They were all too happy to remove as many heads as they could from the shoulders of Japanese soldiers. Here, with the RAF, my father was able to help General Slim's British and Indian soldiers at Kohima. It was tricky flying up from jungle clearings at Imphal north into the Naga Hills, yet RAF Spitfires were able to successfully strafe Japanese troops while C-47s and other transport planes supplied food, artillery pieces and ammunition to the defenders. The Japanese fought with great ferocity, but by 22 June when they gave up, they had lost 80,000 men in and around Kohima. Survivors were racked with dysentery, bloodless from leeches, riddled with worms and starving to death. Many ordinary soldiers, clustered in small gangs over a shared hand-grenade, committed suicide. Officers disembowelled them-selves. Soldiers who had tried to beg, steal or bludgeon food from the hostile, English-speaking Nagas met medieval deaths.

The Battle of Kohima, still largely forgotten today, was the turning point in the Burma campaign. It was described by Lord Mountbatten, the Supreme Allied Commander, South-East Asia, as an act of 'naked unparalleled heroism', and as 'the British-Indian Thermopylae', the legendary ancient battle in which a tiny number of Spartans had stood firm against the Persians and the biggest army the world had ever seen. I dwell on Kohima, not just for sentimental reasons, but because it showed just how important air power was to the success of land armies, and why it was so absurd to have ever believed that India and South-East Asia could be defended by just five squadrons of outmoded aircraft. In the event, fighter sorties aside, the RAF flew 19,000 tons of supplies and 12,000 men into Nagaland during the Battle of Kohima, and flew out 13,000 casualties and 43,000 non-combatants. Spitfires ensured that only three British transport planes were lost throughout the siege. The Japanese, meanwhile, had few suitable long-range aircraft designed to do the same; in any case, those that tried came up against Spitfires.

The Japanese invasion of South-East Asia, and the resulting threat to India, had forced Britain to improve air defences in the region significantly. Between the fall of Singapore in February 1942 and the Battle of Kohima, Buffaloes and Blenheims were replaced by Hurricanes and Mohawks. The number of squadrons grew to forty-eight by mid-1943. Radar-equipped Beaufighters defended Calcutta. The Spitfires, three squadrons of Mk Vs at first, appeared in late 1943, with specially adapted Mk VIIIs arriving in their wake. Pilots faced a new enemy: tropical storms. These could be terrifying. Flying Officer, later Wing Commander, 'Hank' Costain of 615 (County of Surrey) Squadron never forgot the day on 10 August 1944 when he was flying back from the Nagaland front to RAF Baigachi, Calcutta. The squadron found itself approaching a thick brown storm that had usurped the sky. There was no way out, even in a Spitfire. They had to fly through the jaws of a monsoon. 'Within seconds, I was completely out of control and with the artificial horizon toppled, I had not the faintest idea which way was "up". Outside it was so dark that I could not even see my wing tips, and the pounding of the walnut-sized hailstones on the fuselage drowned even the noise of the engine.' Dragged unwillingly up a 10,000-foot current of air, Costain was sent into an equally vicious downdraught. At 1,000 feet he bailed out, fracturing a leg, and came to earth, splashily, in a paddy field. Three of the squadron's twelve Spitfires were lost and their pilots, including the CO, with them. Those aircraft that got back to Baigachi safely had been drawn up through the storm and hurled, thankfully, into clear blue skies above it. 'When it is angry,' Costain wrote, 'the sky is a foe without mercy.'

Other perils for the seven squadrons of Mk VIII Spitfire pilots based in Bengal and then Burma as they made their way in hops, skips and jumps to Rangoon and then on to Singapore included poisonous snakes and foul diseases. They lived in grass huts at Palel during the height of the Battle of Kohima, but at least had the luxury of canvas tents in Burma. In one of these my father met the enemy face to face for the first time; he was writing to my mother when a Japanese infantry officer walked into his tent, sword drawn. Too taken aback to do much, my father looked in horror at the soldier, who then fell to the ground and died; he had been shot by RAF Regiment guards. My father brought the sword back home with him in 1946. It was kept well hidden away when I was a child.

The one squadron of the Royal Indian Air Force (RIAF) to be equipped with Spitfires that flew in action during the war was No. 8, formed in December 1942. It received Spitfires in July 1944, flying sorties during the attempted Japanese invasion and pathfinder missions for Allied Mustangs and Thunderbolts in Burma as well as making supply drops to Burmese guerrillas. Re-equipped with Mk XIVs, the squadron went on to fly Hawker Tempest IIs and, in the years after independence, Soviet jets. Two-seater Harvard trainers, attached to the RAF Spitfire squadrons, meanwhile, were flown as often as they could be spared to Calcutta to bring back gin, tonic and the latest gramophone records. Some of these squadrons were manned, both in the air and on the ground, by veterans of the Battle of Britain. As they flew to bases ever further east, during the course of a long war they fought the Germans, the Italians and now the Japanese.

Spitfire Mk VIIIs of 136 Squadron on Brown's West Island, Indian Ocean, in August 1945.

Japanese pilots had met Spitfires for the first time on Boxing Day, 1943. They got a nasty biff on the nose. A pair of Spits, piloted by Flying Officer Geoffrey William Andrews, a bank clerk from Hamilton, New South Wales, and Flight Sergeant Harry B. Chatfield, a civil servant from Bendigo, took on a swarm of Japanese bombers and fighters over Chittagong that morning. Andrews destroyed a fighter and a bomber, damaging a second, while Chatfield took out another two. He had flown just ten hours on 'ops'. On the last day of 1943, Royal Australian Air Force (RAAF) Spitfires destroyed eleven Japanese bombers and three fighters. From London, Churchill sent a cable complimenting the

Australian squadrons on their 'brilliant exploit', and Sir Archibald Sinclair, Secretary of Air, cabled, 'Clearly the Spitfires have found their way into good hands.' They had.

In massed air battles above Chittagong in 1943–4, Spitfire pilots scored spectacular successes over Japanese bombers, demonstrating to Tokyo that, much like Hitler's Operation Sealion, the invasion of India might have to be postponed after all. Recalling the aerial battle of 1940, Spitfires and Hurricanes flew in tandem to defend India and rebuff the Japanese, although the Hurricanes were, by this stage in the war, used mostly as fighter-bombers. By late 1944, the Japanese Army Air Force had been largely driven away from over Burma, and thus from India too. Spitfires over Chittagong, Kohima and Calcutta had helped to turn the tide. Even so, Spitfire losses were often naggingly high when the aircraft had to fly far out to sea, as the RAAF in particular had discovered while defending Darwin. All too many would run out of fuel over water. The Spitfire had its limitations.

The Australian pilots protecting Darwin were also not helped by the quality of the aircraft they received from Britain and elsewhere. Many of their Mk VC Spitfires, despatched by order of Winston Churchill to Darwin in summer 1942, were the equivalent of clapped-out, second-hand cars. Parts were in short supply. They had, in any case, been previously modified to fly in desert conditions and had not subsequently been remodified for the tropical conditions experienced in and around Darwin. Given these limitations, the Australian pilots did remarkably well, fighting their own Battle of Britain with considerable success against the Japanese. Number 1 Fighter Wing, known as the 'Churchill Wing' and comprising three Spitfire squadrons, commenced action in January 1943. On 2 March, the first occasion they came up against

Japanese Zeros, they shot two down without loss. By the end of the year, the Australian Spitfires had destroyed more than 100 enemy aircraft, and the Japanese abandoned their raids on the Australian mainland. The Wing was re-equipped with brand-new Mk VIIIs in 1944, and later fought in Borneo and elsewhere in the South Pacific.

Back in Europe, the Spitfire was fighting a very different war. Raymond Baxter, better known as the presenter of BBC TV's *Tomorrow's World*, flew Mk XVI Spitfires with 602 Squadron against V2 rocket installations. The V2 was first launched against London from sites in Holland in September 1944, and not even Flight Lieutenant Martindale could have caught up with one in flight. Designed by a team led by the brilliant young German rocket scientist Wernher von Braun, and built with the aid of a great deal of expendable slave labour, the 45-foot-long V2's ballistic trajectory took it up to speeds of 5,000 mph. It was to become the basis of the NASA space programme run by von Braun after the war and the technology it pioneered was to lead directly to Neil Armstrong and 'Buzz' Aldrin, the former a Korean War fighter pilot, becoming the first men to step on the moon on 11 July 1969.

A full quarter of a century before the *Eagle* landed in the Sea of Tranquility, however, all that mattered to Flight Lieutenant Baxter was the V2's destruction. 'During our attacks on a launching site,' he recalls, 'we must have caught the V2 firing crew well into their countdown. After we had released our bombs and were going back for a low-level "strafe" with our cannon, one of the flame-belching monsters began to climb slowly out from a clump of trees. Flight Sergeant "Cupid" Love, one of my pilots, actually fired a long burst at it with his cannon – which must have been the first ever attempt to bring down a ballistic missile in flight.' This was remarkable. Here was a piston-engined fighter, developed in the mid-1930s, taking on the space age; it was almost as if the Spitfire had flown through a time warp.

Down below, though, Allied troops were slogging their way across France and the Low Countries towards the borders of Germany. On D-Day, 6 June 1944, Spitfires, from Mk Vs to Mk XIVs, had flown in massed ranks above the Normandy beaches to assist the Allied landings. Opposition from Field Marshal Erwin Rommel's fortifications was fierce, but the Luftwaffe was almost nowhere to be seen as it was now increasingly held back in defence of the Fatherland itself. The first Allied fighters to land in Normandy, on makeshift airfields, built by, among others, Major Denys Lasdun, future architect of the Royal National Theatre on London's South Bank, were the Spitfire Mk IXBs of 222 Squadron at St Croix-sur-Mer on 10 June. As soon as they touched down, they were refuelled by a Commando unit and flew straight back into action. On 17 July, Spitfire Mk IXBs of Raymond Baxter's 602 Squadron dived on a German staff car scurrying along a Normandy lane and opened fire. Field Marshal Rommel was among the badly wounded.

As Spitfires fresh from England flew in barrels of beer for thirsty troops, the Germans, under the veteran commander Field Marshal von Runstedt, launched their last major offensive against the Allies. In dismal December weather that kept Allied air power grounded, the Germans raced through the Ardennes Forest with some of their old Blitzkrieg spirit. But it was too late. Although under Albert Speer's direction German war production, including that of aircraft, had reached an all-time high in the months leading up to von Runstedt's push, the Reich was coming apart at the seams and its leadership disintegrating. The Luftwaffe did mount one last impressive attack on 1 January 1945, when it sent no fewer than 800 aircraft to attack Allied airfields. Some 200 Allied aircraft, many of them Spitfires, were destroyed or badly damaged on the ground at St Denis-Westren, Maldeghem and Ophoven. But these could be replaced very quickly indeed. The Germans lost some 300 aircraft, fifty-six of them shot down by Spitfires, and 200 pilots killed. It was to be the Luftwaffe's final fling on such an epic scale.

The Germans were still leading the way in jet-fighter – and jet-bomber – technology, just as their aircraft companies were still drawing plans for a bewildering array of futuristic machines, many of which would spur post-war aeronautical developments in Britain, America and Russia. But even when their jets did see action, they often proved vulnerable to the latest generation of Spitfires and their American cousins, the P-51D and P-47D. Meanwhile, Joe Smith and his team at Supermarine offered still further refinements of the Spitfire. The first of the big new Spitfires, the F 21, which had a completely redesigned wing, was now entering service, but only 120 were built. The war in Europe was nearly over.

Out east, Seafires covered the landings at Rangoon and Penang and attacked oil fields in Sumatra. There appeared to be no opposition in the air. On 1 April 1945, Seafires shot down their first kamikazes in the form of three Mitsubishi Zeros converted for the purpose and with their canopies sealed to ensure their pilots could not bail out. Seafires were readied for the invasion of Japan, but the nuclear bombs dropped from high-flying, pressurized Boeing B-29 Superfortresses on Hiroshima and Nagasaki in August 1945 brought an end to the conflict in the Pacific. On their last day of action in the Second World War – 15 August – Seafires destroyed eight Zero fighters for no loss.

It had been a remarkable war for the Spitfire. It had come through six years of fighting as not just a frontline fighter but the British frontline fighter. It had done pretty much everything asked of it. Only at the very end of the war was the Navy seriously interested in the Seafang, the seagoing model of Supermarine's new Spiteful piston-engined fighter, and this was mainly because the Admiralty expected that it would be fighting against Japan well into 1946. But an altogether novel form of warfare, one unimagined by R. J. Mitchell, had put a quick end to Japanese resistance. And, in effect, to the piston-engined fighter. A new aerial world order of V-bombers and Mach-2 interceptors was in the offing. Even so, the Spitfire's days were far from over. It had performed so very well that both the RAF and the Royal Navy, as well as many other air forces around the world, ordered the latest generation of Spitfires even after the Japanese surrender. Remarkably, the descendants of R. J. Mitchell's Type 300 would still be flying with the RAF for another six years, and with the Royal Navy for another nine. By the end of the Second World War, the Spitfire had seen off Messerschmitts, Focke-Wulfs, Macchis, Nakajimas and Mitsubishis, and had even had a crack at flying bombs and the world's first operational jet fighter and ballistic missile. It was far from ready to come down to land.

CHAPTER IV

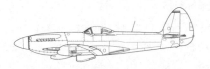

THE LONG GOODBYE

BLUE Spitfires. Pink Spitfires. White Spitfires. Yellow Spitfires. Spitfires with wings striped like zebra crossings. Spitfires adorned with roundels, red stars, and even, when captured, swastikas. The Second World War had witnessed Mitchell's masterpiece in coats of many colours. But a glossy black Spitfire? Surely no air force would ever have considered painting a fighter such a light-catching colour? It would stand out against the backdrop of any sky like a Montgolfier balloon over late eighteenth-century Paris or a bird of paradise today on a grey morning in Kensington Gardens.

In 2005, a lone glossy black Spitfire flew over the funeral cortège of Ezer Weizman, former president of Israel. Its flight marked one end of a long, extraordinarily complex and painful story. Born in Tel Aviv in 1924, Weizman was a nephew of Israel's first president, Chaim Weizmann, and brother-in-law of the famous Israeli soldier and politician Moshe Dayan. In the Second World War, which he began as a lorry driver in the Western Desert campaigns with the British Eighth Army, Weizman went on, after training in Southern Rhodesia, to fly Spitfires with the RAF in India. In the Israeli War of Independence of 1948–9, he

The glossy black Spitfire Mk IX formerly flown by Israeli fighter pilot and president Ezer Weizman.

was a fighter pilot again, but this time fighting the Egyptians, together with the Syrians, Jordanians and Iraqis, as well as the Arab Liberation and Holy War armies.

The Holy War Army was the child of Muhammed Amin al-Husseini, the Mufti of Jerusalem and a former artillery officer in the First World War Ottoman army, whose fight against the establishment of a Jewish state had caused him to ally himself with Hitler in 1933. Al-Husseini sought approval from Berlin for the formation of a National Socialist Arab Party in Palestine, and later recruited Muslims into a specially formed Waffen-SS regiment. In May 1941, he promoted the divinely approved Axis cause in the Middle East by issuing a fatwa, from exile in Iraq, for a holy war against Britain. On 2 November 1943, he received a telegram from Heinrich Himmler: 'In the recognition of this enemy [international Jewry] and of the common struggle against it lies the firm foundation of the natural alliance that exists between the National Socialist Greater Germany and the freedom-loving Muslims of the whole world.'

Small wonder, then, that Weizman chose to fly a Spitfire against his Arab enemies in 1948–9. If only, though, the story had been as simple as a clear-cut fight between Israeli pilots equipped with the liberating Spitfire and a pro-Nazi Arab enemy supplied with tainted German weapons. In reality it was much more complex. During the labyrinthine course of the Israeli War of Independence, Weizman flew a Spitfire against similar machines of both the Royal Egyptian Air Force (REAF) and the RAF. RAF Spitfire squadrons, fired on by both sides, were caught in the middle of this unholy mess as Britain attempted to police the Arab-Jewish conflict and broker a settlement. Israel won the war convincingly.

This was the last military action in which Spitfires were shot down in aerial combat. One of these, early in the conflict, had been a Mk IX of the REAF; the damaged aircraft was recovered by the Israelis, rebuilt and sent back into action against its former owners. This was Weizman's personal Spitfire. After the war, it was restored and painted glossy black. Weizman flew it, as a kind of mascot, company plane and perhaps even as a provocation, during the years 1958 to 1966, when he was head of the Israeli Air Force (IAF). The aircraft remains Israeli state property and is kept in perfect flying order.

The Israelis had been desperately keen to get their hands on Spitfires. Two, including Weizman's, were sourced in the Middle East. A further thirteen Mk IXs were purchased from the Czechs who, in turn, had bought them from the British at the end of the Second World War. Because they could only be delivered to the

Israelis secretly, they were dispatched in two undercover missions. Refuelling could only take place in Yugoslavia, and every last bit of unnecessary equipment was stripped from the aircraft. This included radios and compasses, except in the flight leaders' planes. In these circumstances, it was remarkable that as many as thirteen of the Spitfires flown from Czechoslovakia during 1948 reached the Promised Land. Czech Spitfires were also sent by sea, but they arrived too late to fight.

To make matters more complicated, the first aircraft Weizman (who had studied aeronautics in England in 1946–7) flew in combat with the Sherut Avir, precursor of the IAF, was not British, nor even American, but an Avia S-199. This was, more or less – with an emphasis on the less, a Messerschmitt Bf 109G built under licence in Czechoslovakia and powered, or rather underpowered, by a Jumo 211F bomber engine. How odd that the Israelis should have flown an aircraft that had been such a potent symbol of Nazi aggression. But it was a matter of expediency: the Israelis flew anything they could get their hands on and they could shoot the enemy down with. Weizman flew in Israel's very first fighter mission, a ground attack on an Egyptian column advancing towards Tel Aviv near the Arab town of Isdud. He also flew in the last aerial combat of the war, on 7 January 1949, when four Israeli Mk IXs engaged a force of fourteen RAF Mk XVIII Spitfires and Hawker Tempest Mk Vs after an earlier flight of RAF Spitfires on a reconnaissance mission had infringed Israel's southern border. The IAF claimed three Mk XVIIIs destroyed. Spitfires had thus fought and destroyed Spitfires: the Israelis had shot down the very machines that had done so much to liberate European Jews.

The RAF seemed to accept this unsettling turn of events with remarkably good grace. In 1951, Weizman attended courses at the

RAF Staff and Command College in England, before returning to Israel to become commander of the first IAF unit to fly Gloster Meteor jets, supplied, of course, from Britain. Even stranger at the time, though, was the fact that many of the fighter pilots flying for the proto-IAF in 1948–9 were not, like Weizman, Israeli-born and bred. They were drawn from fifteen countries and formed 70 per cent of Israeli pilots; no fewer than 181 had flown in the Second World War. Of the thirty-three Israeli pilots who died in the War of Independence, nineteen were foreigners: eight Americans, six Canadians, three Britons and two South Africans. Perhaps this was hardly surprising as, following a ban on their recruitment until late in 1943, there were only twenty-five qualified Palestinian Jewish RAF pilots by the end of the Second World War.

The Syrian Air Force, meanwhile, may well have included a number of former Luftwaffe pilots, who flew American Harvard trainers against Czech-built Bf 109Gs flown by American Jews. The first major air action in the war had been on 22 May 1948, when a squadron of Mk IX Spitfires of the REAF attacked, by mistake, the RAF base at Ramat David shared by 32 and 208 Squadrons. They destroyed a number of Mk XVIII Spitfires on the ground. Up went the surviving RAF Spitfires in hot pursuit, with those of Roy Bowie, Geoff Cooper and Tim McElhaw bringing down four of the five Egyptian raiders. Later, the American pilot Chalmers Goodlin, flying an Israeli Mk IX, was to shoot down Cooper's Mk XVIII. Two other American pilots, Gideon Lichtmann and Rudolph Augarten, flying *faux* Bf 109Gs, both brought down REAF Mk IX Spitfires. The REAF, meanwhile, fought the Israelis not just with Mk IX Spitfires but former Regia Aeronautica Macchi MC 205s. As it was, at least two REAF Spitfires were put out of action by rival Israeli Mk IXs flown by British-born pilots, while the recently pro-Nazi Iraqis made a poor showing all round with a motley fleet of clapped-out Messerschmitt Bf 110s, Heinkel He 111s and Fiat CR 42 biplanes.

The aerial war had been as confusing as the events surrounding the building of the biblical Tower of Babel. All Israeli pilots, Palestinian-born or not, who flew in the War of Independence or what Arabs refer to as 'al Nakba', the catastrophe, spoke English over their radio transmitters: only a handful were able to speak Hebrew. In that last combat on 7 January 1949, however, the nascent IAF had proved itself a force to be reckoned with. Within a few years, Weizman, a Spitfire enthusiast, had built the IAF into an efficient and lethal military machine, as the course of future wars between Israel and her Arab neighbours was to prove. And yet, like so many other Spitfire pilots, he was no warmonger. From the late 1970s, he rejected the doctrine of a 'Greater Israel' and called for peace talks with both Egypt and Yasser Arafat's Palestine Liberation Organization. The glossy black 1940s fighter that flew over his funeral procession in 2005 was, if such a down-to-earth metaphor could ever be pinned to the tail of a Spitfire, a sword wielded in desert skies and reconstructed into a most elegant ploughshare.

The Israeli War of Independence was just one of many combats Mitchell's fighter took part in during the decade following the end of the Second World War. All of them proved to be fights in, or over, countries struggling to kick off the yoke of empire, whether British, Dutch or French. None, except perhaps the Israeli war, offered much of an opportunity for the Spitfire to shine. There was nothing glorious in strafing the supposed positions of communist guerrillas in Far Eastern jungles, nor was the Spitfire an ideal machine for such missions.

A Seafire Mk 47 of 800 Squadron operating from the aircraft carrier HMS Triumph in 1950.

There were, in these years, two quite different generations of Spitfires, and Seafires, flying in action. There were those representing the ultimate development of the Mitchell-Smith breed, such as the RAF's fine F 24 Spitfires and the Royal Navy's Mk 47 Seafires, and there were those bought second-hand by emerging countries in search of an air force on the cheap. By the time of the Japanese surrender, thousands of redundant Spitfires were parked on Allied airfields, many of them brand-new. They were made available to buyers at favourable rates. The air force of Nationalist China had been among those that had tried to buy Spitfires before the Second World War: it badly needed a modern fighter to take on the Japanese. The outbreak of war between Britain and Germany had, understandably, scuppered any deal, and by the time the Chinese renewed their interest, their country was now officially communist. As the Iron Curtain had divided both Europe and East and West, the Chinese made their representation to the Soviets. No one seems to know quite what transpired, but a number of the surviving Mk IXs exported to the Soviet Union during the war made their way to China. The fate of the Chinese Spitfires still appears to be a military secret.

In 1950, a far less controversial sale of fifty unused Griffon-powered Mk XIX reconnaissance machines was made to the Swedish Air Force. Ironically, these replaced the very high-flying German Junkers Ju 86K that the Spitfire had proved well able to shoot down during the Second World War. A handsome deep-blue Mk XIX, designated an S-31, can still be seen in company with a P-51D Mustang and a gaggle of indigenous Saab piston-engined fighters at the Swedish Air Force Museum, Malmslatt.

Of the seventy-seven Mk IXs sold to Czechoslovakia in 1945, and flown there until 1951, a large number had been sold on to Israel in 1948–9. Of the Israeli survivors, some thirty were then re-exported in 1954–5 to Burma, where they joined the air force's twenty Seafire XVs, purchased in 1952 direct from Vickers-Armstrong, and three Mk XVIII Spitfires bought in 1948 from Air Command South-East Asia, to strafe communist positions in the north of the country as civil war replaced the struggle between the British and Japanese. The accident rate amongst Spitfire pilots in Burma was, unfortunately, exceptionally high.

Spitfires also flew on into the first decade of the jet age with the air forces of Denmark, Greece, India, Italy, the Netherlands, Norway, Portugal, South Africa, Southern Rhodesia, Syria, Turkey and Yugoslavia, as well as with the Irish Air Corps and the Hong Kong Auxiliary Air Force. In the Turkish Air Force, they even flew alongside veteran Fw 190s. At least one Syrian Spitfire was destroyed on the ground by the IAF as late as 1967, but presumably this was a squadron mascot or a machine that had been either mothballed or otherwise preserved.

The biggest users of the Spitfire and the Seafire for most of this period were the RAF and Fleet Air Arm. Both continued to take delivery of the latest variants of the Supermarine fighters until well into 1948. They had good reason to do so. The development of the piston-engined fighter was coming to an end and so there was no need to invest in some untried, late-flowering design when the military jet was on its way. Yet the very latest Spitfires were well up to scratch, being in many ways faster, except in straight and level flight, and more manoeuvrable than the early jet fighters. And these beautiful machines were still the forces' sweethearts – it would be hard for them to part for good with their favourite aircraft. Remarkably then, the all-metal Spitfire was both the first of its type in service with the RAF and the last. It defined the era of the long-nosed, liquid-cooled, piston-engined fighter; it saw the era in and saw it out.

Development of the Spitfire had continued right up until the end of the Second World War and even beyond. However, the story might have turned out differently if the Supermarine Type 393, the Victory but later named the Spiteful, had tipped its older sibling from the late wartime sky. The Spiteful – a stupid sort of name – was developed from 1942 using a Spitfire fuselage, a Griffon engine and thin and stubby laminar-flow wings like those of the highly successful North American Mustang P-51D. Supermarine engineers believed – mistakenly, as it transpired – that this type of wing would prove to be superior to the Spitfire's elliptical wing at very high speeds. It would also be easier to make, install, repair and replace, and would allow for a wider and outwards-retracting undercarriage, something which promised to make Spiteful landings much easier than those made by Spitfires.

The new wing was tried first on a modified Mk XIV Spitfire, flown by Jeffrey Quill three weeks after D-Day. The Spiteful was faster than a Mk XIV, but Quill found it much less forgiving as it approached the stall. Even so, once the wing had been married to a new, custom-designed fuselage, the RAF placed orders for 150 of the machines through the Air Ministry. Was the Spitfire out of favour? Not quite, but almost. Problems with the first F 21 Spitfires encouraged the Air Fighting Development Unit to recommend that not only should the new mark be withdrawn immediately from service, but also that all development on the Spitfire should cease. The problems with the F 21 were resolved, however, and it was the Spiteful that took a dive, not its evergreen predecessor. In any case, with the arrival of the Gloster Meteor jet in 1944, there seemed to be no point in pursuing the new project. The Spitfire might as well keep up its excellent work until overtaken by the new jets. And it did.

Some of the less well-known developments later in the war included the commissioning of a pair of hi-tech Spitfire fuselages made of Aerolite. This was a composite material invented by the Chilean-born and Cambridge-educated inventor Norman de Bruyne, who had learned to fly in a De Havilland Moth in 1931. That same year, he set up the Cambridge Aeroplane Construction Company, which became Aero Research Ltd in 1934. De Bruyne designed and built his own aircraft, the Snark, from stressed plywood and phenol-formaldehyde resins. It flew, successfully, a year before Mitchell's aluminium Spitfire. To be precise, the Spitfire was largely made of duraluminium, or aluminium alloyed with copper, manganese and magnesium, a material invented by the German metallurgist Alfred Wilm in 1909 and used in the construction of the Zeppelins that bombed England in the First

World War. During the early 1940s, De Bruyne developed the first reinforced composite material, Aerolite, a flax-reinforced phenol-formaldehyde resin initially used by the military in the construction of the tail planes of Miles Magister trainers and wing spars of Bristol Blenheim bombers. A lightweight Spitfire made of composites would have solved the problem of the dire aluminium shortage predicted for 1944. But this never happened and the Aerolite fuselages were never made up into complete aircraft. De Bruyne's research was nonetheless far from wasted; it became the basis of new construction methods and materials in the post-war British and international aircraft industries. It had all been an intriguing proposition and, once again, the Spitfire was more than keeping pace with the times.

The Royal Navy, meanwhile, was keen on the Spiteful. It believed, especially given the painfully long take-off runs needed by first-generation jets, that the decks of its aircraft carriers were too short for anything but piston-engined aircraft. As a result, it ordered a naval version of the Spiteful, which was launched as the Seafang – another rather silly name. With its folding wings and six-bladed contra-rotating propeller, the prototype Seafang, a converted Spiteful XV, certainly looked the part. But with the first successful flight of the De Havilland Sea Vampire jet from the deck of HMS *Ocean* taking place in December 1945, the Seafang was completely redundant.

As it was, twenty-two Spitefuls were built, in three marks, and eighteen Seafangs. With a 2,420-hp Griffon 121 engine, the Spiteful F XVI weighed less than late-mark Spitfires and was designed for a top speed, in level flight, of 494 mph. Did one ever fly so very fast? Perhaps; perhaps not. This was almost, but not quite, the end of the Spiteful's story. In late 1943, Supermarine's

Joe Smith began to work on a jet version of the aircraft. It was to be powered by the new Rolls-Royce Nene engine. Thinking, perhaps, that a jet Spitfire was in the making, the Air Ministry issued a specification, E.10/44, the following year. The prototype, the Jet Spiteful, TS409, made its maiden flight on 27 July 1946. Sadly, it was not a significant improvement on the new De Havilland Vampire, so nothing came of it. The Navy, though, was interested, and Smith's jet finally emerged as the short-lived Supermarine Attacker, which was capable of 590 mph and served with the Fleet Air Arm from 1951 to 1954.

Production of the Spitfire, and of the Merlin and Griffon engines, continued after the Japanese surrender in August 1945, in part to keep the cogs of Britain's aircraft industry spinning. Eventually, a grand total of 22,789 Spitfires were built. Even then, by the end of the following year, just two home frontline RAF squadrons, 41 with F 21s and 63 with Mk XIVs, were still equipped with Spitfires. In June 1946, however, the Royal Auxiliary Air Force was reformed with thirteen Spitfire squadrons. The last RAF Spitfire squadron left occupied Germany in 1949; this was 80 Squadron, which took its new F 24s, the last of the many Spitfire marks, on to its base at Kai-Tak airport, Hong Kong. Although the squadron was re-equipped with the beautiful twin-piston-engined De Havilland Hornet at the beginning of 1952, several of its F 24 Spitfires stayed on with the Hong Kong Auxiliary Air Force until 21 April 1955, when one of the aircraft performed a last fly-past on the occasion of the Queen's birthday.

The F 24 looked quite unlike the K5054 or the Battle of Britain's Mk I and II. As the RAF Museum, Hendon, says, 'It is perhaps a mark of the propaganda value of the Spitfire name that this very different machine was not renamed.' How different was it? Its wing was all new. Its fuselage was cut down with a blister canopy offering all-round vision. The tail was new, much larger and adopted from the Spiteful. The engine cowling was thrust even further forward to shroud the latest version of the Rolls-Royce Griffon. Much had been done with this, the last of the line, to give the Spitfire back something of its graceful handling, although the F 24 was designed primarily for ground attack. This took a lot of doing, and along the way the F 24 had effectively developed into a different aircraft from Mitchell's original. Just fifty-four were built, most of them going straight into store. I wish they were still there, and that I had the key.

The last RAF Spitfires based in Japan, Mk XIVs of 17 Squadron, Iwakuni, were withdrawn in early 1948. But RAF Spitfires based in the Far East were still to see action when the Malayan Emergency was declared in May 1948. Despite the name, this was a full-blown guerrilla war fought over twelve long years between British, Commonwealth and Malaysian forces against the Malayan Races Liberation Army (MRLA). Created by the Malayan Communist Party (MCP), the MRLA was formed mostly of Chinese Malays who had fought loyally with the British against the Japanese occupation during the Second World War. Because of this, the British granted legal recognition to the MCP. The MCP, though, was impatient for an independent Malaya. On 16 June 1948 its soldiers killed three British rubber-planters at Sungai Siput, Perak. The British declared a state of emergency. On 6 July the Mk XVIIIs of 81 Squadron struck with rockets, largely destroying an MCP camp. From February 1949, Spitfires began dropping 20-lb fragmentation bombs. The most intense attacks on enemy targets, or what British pilots liked to call 'Charlie Tango', airspeak for communist terrorists, were made in late 1949; on 21 October, RAF Spitfires and Seafires from 800 Squadron flew sixty-two sorties.

'I vividly remember the first time I dropped a bomb in anger,' recalled Flying Officer Nicholson of 28 Squadron, later Air Marshal Sir John Nicholson. 'On 2 July 1948, I went off with my squadron commander, Squadron Leader Bob Yule [from RAF Sembawang, Singapore Island], to a target just across the causeway from Singapore, in South Jahore. We took off at first light so that we could get in our dive attacks before the usual mid-morning layer of cumulus cloud developed. When we reached the target area, we cruised around for more than half an hour looking for something resembling our briefed objective, before eventually we did attack. Diving from 12,000 feet, we dropped our 500-pounders, two from each aircraft, then we carried out a series of strafing runs with cannon and machine-guns. There was nobody firing back; it was really like being on the range – except that the target was far less distinct.'

The sixteen Spitfires from the two frontline squadrons based in Singapore did their bit against the advance of communism by flying some 1,800 sorties over Malaya. Guerrilla fighters had been forced to move from camp to camp, never knowing when the RAF fighters would come growling down low above the trees, cannon blazing. And yet, as John Nicholson and his fellow pilots recognized at the time, the Spitfires were never exactly at home in this climate nor with this type of guerrilla jungle warfare. Fairly early on, a problem with electrical wiring meant they were banned from carrying rockets, while over the months their serviceability rate fell to around 50 per cent. Pilots were often unsure if they were simply shooting up trees rather than communist strongholds. The last offensive sorties made by RAF Spitfires were flown by the

Mk XVIIIs of 60 Squadron over Malaya on 1 January 1951. The last of all was led by Wing Commander Wilfrid Duncan Smith. Immaculately restored, the Spitfire he flew that day, TP280, flies today in the United States.

The Malayan Emergency was later overshadowed by both the Korean War and the conflict in Indo-China which saw the French defeated by the Vietnamese. Yet it had been a very real war with some 35,000 British and Commonwealth and 100,000 Malayan troops pitted against 80,000 MCP guerrillas. At least 6,710 communist soldiers were killed, together with 519 British military personnel and 1,346 Malayan soldiers. Independence from Britain in August 1957 robbed the MCP of its purpose, although it continued to fight on regardless for at least another year, before disbanding or disappearing across the jungle border into Thailand. The Malayan government, under Prime Minister Tunku Abdul Rahman, declared the Emergency over in July 1960.

Spitfires were not required to fight in the Korean War, but Seafires were. HMS *Triumph*, a Colossus-class light fleet aircraft carrier, was the only Royal Navy ship of her type on duty in the Far East in the early months of the war. Her complement included the Seafire Mk 47s of 800 Squadron as well as Fairey Fireflies. The Mk 47s were fine flying and fighting machines, with 2,200-hp Griffon 87 engines driving a six-bladed contra-rotating prop, hydraulic folding wings, bubble canopies, the big and very efficient Spiteful tail-section and a top speed of 452 mph. Arriving on the scene at the very end of piston-engined fighter development, just ninety were built, the last being delivered into squadron service in March 1949. The Mk 47 flew for the last time in service with 764 Training Squadron on 23 November 1954.

HMS *Triumph*'s twelve Seafires were sent on their first sortie, together with nine Fireflies, on a raid against Haeju airfield on the west coast of Korea on 3 July 1950. But again, like their F 24 Spitfire counterparts, and like all Spitfires before them, they were hampered by their short range. Because they were still not as tough as naval aircraft ought to be, they suffered badly when landing heavily back on board, especially on days of heavy seas. By the end of the month, after flying 245 offensive patrols and 115 ground attacks, 800 Squadron was down to three serviceable Seafires. Inevitably, the Seafire Mk 47's operational life had been a short one.

Griffon-engined Seafires, starting with the Mk XV, had arrived at the very end of the Second World War and just too late to see active service. With the enormous torque developed by the 37-litre V12, they had not been the easiest of aircraft to fly from carrier decks. They would, though, have been one of the few aircraft able to tackle successfully the Yokosuka MXY7 Ohka, or Cherry Blossom, kamikaze rocket plane. The tiny Ohka, packing a powerful 1,200-kg explosive punch, was designed by Ensign Mitsuo Ohta, a transport pilot with the Japanese Navy, and developed with the Aeronautical Research Institute at Tokyo University. Dropped some twenty miles away at 27,000 feet from the belly of a twin-engined Mitsubishi G4M Betty bomber, the Ohka would glide, nose down, towards its target at 230 mph. Three miles out, it would dive, rocket motors ignited, at somewhere between 500 and 600 mph. Ohka pilots appear to have sunk fifteen US ships, causing great loss of life. If the war had not been brought to a sudden conclusion, there would have been a new and much more deadly second-generation Ohka jet to undertake suicide missions. The Seafire XV would, timed correctly, have been able to dive at 500 mph or more against these single-sortie aircraft; and it might have proved a great help in the last push against Japan. As it was, it was overtaken by events.

After the war, the French Aeronavale and the Royal Canadian Navy flew Seafire Mk XVIIs, the latter until April 1954. Meanwhile Spitfires continued to serve with the RAF post-Malaya on photo-reconnaissance missions; the last was made by a PR Mk XIX on 1 April 1954. Even after this, three PR XIXs were kept in service with the RAF's meteorological Temperature and Humidity Flight, making over 4,000 flights before being replaced by twin-engined De Havilland Mosquitoes in June 1957. These Spitfires would become the basis of the RAF's Battle of Britain Memorial Flight.

The Indian Air Force, which used Spitfires in action in the battles of Badgam and Shelatang during Partition, when Pakistan, a separate Muslim state, was split away from India in 1947, finally phased out what remained of a 159-strong fleet of mostly Mk VIII and PR XI and XIX Spitfires in 1957–8. The Spitfire had finally retired from its role as a warrior. Other air force-owned Spitfires did fly occasionally elsewhere after this, but their role had changed

A Spitfire PR XIX over Malaya: the mark's final mission was flown on 1 April 1954.

from that of frontline fighter to mascot and plaything. And yet, how remarkable that the first truly modern British monoplane fighter, first flown from Hampshire at the very height of the age of appeasement, should still have been hard at work, often low down over ocean and jungle, in the jet, nuclear and NATO age. The Spitfire had been a warrior for all seasons, and had fought around the world. Well before its retirement, it had become a symbol of freedom – and a legend.

CHAPTER V

FIRST AMONG EQUALS

THE Spitfire was the finest all-round fighter of its time. It was beautiful but it was not perfect, and in certain theatres of war and operations it had its limitations. It also had its rivals, friends and foes alike. On the other hand, the Seafire should not really be compared to the superb purpose-built carrier fighters of the United States Navy and Marine Corps such as the Grumman F6F Hellcat and Vought F4U Corsair, it was a compromise. The wonder of it is that it did its job so well.

That the Spitfire itself did not just perform well but brilliantly in action goes without saying. It was, more or less, the perfect piston-engined fighter. It flew superbly; its controls were light and direct but not over-sensitive; its performance was rarely less than terrific. It packed sufficient punch from its guns, had just about enough armour and was easy to land. It was a fine trade-off, as all fighters must be, of speed, power, agility, firepower, weight, range, ease of maintenance and reliability. Although the Spitfire was fast and powerful, it was not so very difficult for a novice to clamber

The first Griffon-engined Spitfire Mk XIVE on a test flight in the spring of 1944.

aboard and fly it reasonably well. No fighter aircraft has ever been 100 per cent perfect, yet the Spitfire came close. Even then, there were differences between its many marks. The outstanding variants were, I suppose, the Mk I, V, IX, XIV, PR XIX and F 22/24. If you were fighting in Burma or the South Pacific, however, the Mk VIII would have been your first choice. The Spitfire did have its Achilles heels, yet they did little to hold it back in combat, and most were cured well before the final defeat of the Axis powers in 1945.

The taut and tiny Messerschmitt Bf 109 revolutionized the design of fighter aircraft. It was the most advanced machine of its type when it first flew in September 1935, six months ahead of the Spitfire. It was the first to feature an all-metal monocoque construction, a closed canopy and retractable landing gear. It was manufactured throughout the Second World War. In fact, more Bf 109s were built than any other fighter before or since. The total number made is uncertain, with figures ranging from 29,155 to 33,675. Remarkably, no fewer than 12,807 of these were produced in 1944.

The Bf 109 took many British observers by surprise when it went into action with the Luftwaffe's Condor Legion during the Spanish Civil War. How had the Germans, banned by the Treaty of Versailles from designing and making military aircraft, managed to produce the world's most modern fighter so very quickly? After all, the Luftwaffe itself had only been formed in 1935. The answer lay in a combination of intelligence and guile. To counteract the provisions of the 1919 treaty, the German aircraft industry took to developing so-called sports aircraft, many of which were used to develop and test ideas and components that would make their way when the time was propitious into the design of new military machines. Pilots, meanwhile, were trained using high-specification gliders and fast mail planes, which were permitted after 1922. A clandestine base at Lipetsk in the Soviet Union was also established to test purely military designs in return for the training of VVS aircrews. The German government was also able to direct aircraft design and production by creating a single state airline, Luft Hansa.

One of the most successful of the German sports aircraft of the mid-1930s was the fast, agile and pretty four-seat Bf 108 Taifun or Typhoon, first flown in 1934. Willy Emil Messerschmitt and his team used it as the design platform for the Bf 109. Because of the lack of a suitable German engine, the first Bf 109 was powered by a 695-hp Rolls-Royce Kestrel VI motor. Even so, the new fighter from the Bayerische Flugzeugwerke, Augsburg, greatly impressed the Luftwaffe. It was to become the new German Air Force's standard fighter. The son of a wine merchant, Messerschmitt had begun working on the construction of gliders under Friedrich Harth at a military flying school during the First World War, and he was ever after concerned with designing aircraft that were as light as possible. The bantam-weight Bf 109 was the result of a competition held for a new fighter. Only some while after the Bayerische Flugzeugwerke was renamed Messerschmitt did the official designation of the fighter change from Bf to Me 109. Both Luftwaffe and RAF pilots knew the aircraft as the Me 109 throughout the Second World War.

In October 1935, the first fuel-injected Jumo 210-engined Bf 109 flew. In May 1936, the third aircraft emerged from Augsburg with armament installed. Official tests at Travemunde on the Baltic coast were carried out in the summer against the competing Arado Ar 80, Focke-Wulf Fw 159 and Heinkel He 112. Not only was the Bf 109 the fastest of the four, but news from England of the success of the Spitfire, which resembled Messerschmitt's design in many respects, prompted its ordering. The Bf 109B entered service with the Luftwaffe in the spring of 1937; it was soon in action, flying with the Condor Legion during the Spanish Civil War. While young Luftwaffe pilots were learning important lessons in frontline combat, the Bf 109 was wowing audiences at air shows across Europe in its role as aerial ambassador for Nazi Germany. By September 1939, at least 1,000 Bf 109s were ready for the attack on Poland.

The Bf 109 had its faults. Like the Spitfire, it had a short range. Its cockpit was cramped and the track of its undercarriage very narrow indeed. Like the Spitfire's, its wheels retracted outwards, but in Mitchell's design the undercarriage legs were mounted in the wings rather than in the fuselage, thus ensuring the track was that bit wider. In theory, the German installation was very practical: the wings of a Bf 109 could be removed for servicing while the fuselage of the aircraft stood unsupported. But in practice it meant that landing the Bf 109 was always going to be a decidedly iffy business – one that was to lead to many unnecessary injuries and deaths.

The Bf 109E 'Emil' that fought Spitfires in the Battle of Britain was powered by a 1,100-hp Daimler-Benz 601A engine and equipped with two 7.92-mm machine-guns and two 20-mm cannon. A cannon firing through the nose was tried, but although this was to be an exciting feature for future generations of model-makers, in practice it caused severe and disturbing reverberation through the airframe. The 109E was able to out-climb and out-dive the Spitfire, and with its Handley Page wing slats flew extremely well close to the stall, yet overall it could be outmanoeuvred by Mitchell's fighter, which was also the faster of the two at medium and high altitudes. Honours, however, were very much even in practice.

The Bf 109F 'Friedrich', probably the best of the series from the pilot's point of view, boasted improved streamlining, rounded wing tips and a more powerful 1,350-hp Daimler-Benz motor. To keep up with the development of Allied fighters, Messerschmitt developed the beefy Bf 109G 'Gustav', a 1,475-hp machine that, although it carried a heavier armament than ever before, inevitably weighed more than its predecessors and lacked their grace in the air. There were very many variations of the 109G; production continued to the end, by which time some aircraft were fitted with wooden tails as shortages of metal became acute. The 109Bs that flew in Spain could reach 279 mph, the Battle of Britain 109Es 354 mph, the sleek 109Fs 390 mph and the bulky 109Gs 387 mph. The last, highly rationalized model, the Bf 109K 'Kurfurst', had a top speed of 445 mph.

Like the Spitfire, the Bf 109, a Fritz of all trades, was to be pressed into service on the high seas. It had been the intention to fly a version with extended wing area from the deck of the *Graf Zeppelin* aircraft carrier, but this was never completed and the denavalized 109Ts were instead sent to fight in Norway. As it was, the Bf 109 proved a very capable fighter and fighter-bomber which fought in every European theatre as well as in Russia, the Mediterranean and North Africa. Without doubt, the most fascinating version of the fighter was a twin-fuselage, twin-engined design, the Bf 109Z 'Zwilling', but only one of these five-cannon fighter-bombers was built and it never flew.

Bf 109s were also flown by the air forces of Bulgaria, Croatia, Finland, Hungary, Italy, Romania, Slovakia, Switzerland and Yugoslavia. The Japanese received a single machine for evaluation purposes, while the Russians flew captured examples. After the war, as we have seen, Czechoslovak-built Avia S-199 fighters, which were modified Bf 109G-14s, fought with the emergent Israeli Air Force against RAF and REAF Spitfires. In Czechoslovakia, they were replaced in frontline service by Soviet jets in 1952, but flew on as trainers for another five years. In Spain, 109G-2s, known as the Hispano Ha-1112 'Buchon', were built under licence at Seville, initially with Hispano-Suiza and later, ironically, with Rolls-Royce Merlin engines until as late as 1956. A fair few were still in active service until the late 1960s. After that, they were much in demand for film work. Veteran Bf 109s flew on in Finland, Romania and Switzerland into the 1950s.

The German ace Adolf Galland in 1940, when he flew the Messerschmitt Bf 109E.

The RAF had flown a captured Bf 109E from Boscombe Down and Farnborough from May 1940 onwards. It took part in exhaustive mock dogfights with Spitfires, and the results were finally discussed at a meeting of the Royal Aeronautical Society in

London in March 1944. From the British perspective, the Bf 109 had its good points. Among these were its high top speed and excellent rate of climb, good control at slow speed, a gentle stall and the fact that the engine kept running under negative g. Its bad points were heavy ailerons and elevator at speed, high wing loading that caused stalls under g, a poor turning circle, the absence of a rudder trimmer, curtailing its ability to bank left in a dive, and – something very obvious to Hermann Goering, who was unable to fit inside one – that notoriously small cockpit. 'There is no doubt,' concluded the report, 'that in the autumn of 1940 the Bf 109E, in spite of its faults, was a doughty opponent to set against our own equipment.' Or, as Gunther Rall, the Luftwaffe ace with 275 kills to his credit, once put it: 'The 109? That was a dream, the *non plus ultra*. Just like the F-14 of today. Of course, everyone wanted to fly it as soon as possible.'

While RAF Spitfire pilots had got the measure of the Bf 109 during the Battle of Britain, nothing prepared them for the Focke-Wulf Fw 190, an altogether more accomplished and fearsome foe. The Fw 190 Wurger (shrike, or butcher bird) appeared as if out of the sun and from nowhere in the spring of 1942. Clearly superior to the Bf 109, it was also more deadly than the Spitfire Mk V. The arrival of this superb BMW radial-engined fighter forced Joseph Smith and his team at Supermarine to accelerate the pace of the development of the Spitfire at full boost and throttle. For the best part of a year, and until the arrival of the Spitfire Mk IX, the Fw 190 commanded the skies. 'The Focke-Wulf 190 certainly gave the British a shock,' wrote Douglas Bader in his autobiography *Fight for the Sky*; 'it out-climbed and out-dived the Spitfire. Now for the first time the Germans were out-flying our pilots.' They were also out-gunning them.

Luckily for the British, a Luftwaffe pilot landed an Fw 190A, intact, in South Wales in June 1942. Subsequent analysis of this potent machine led not only to the development of the Mk IX Spitfire, but also to Air Ministry specification F.2/43, prompting the design of the powerful Hawker Fury, which was, however, too late to fight in the Second World War.

The Fw 190 story began in the autumn of 1937, when the Reichsluftministerium placed an order with the Focke-Wulf Flugzeugbau, Bremen, for a fighter to supplement the Bf 109. The company's chief engineer and test pilot was Kurt Waldemar Tank, who had previously worked for Albatros until the bankrupt company was merged with Focke-Wulf in 1931. Before the war, Tank designed the elegant Fw 200 Condor, which, along with the Douglas DC-3, was one of the world's first modern monoplane airliners. Condors flew the Atlantic non-stop; they were used during the war as long-range maritime bombers and reconnaissance aircraft.

Going against the grain of contemporary European practice, Tank based the design of the Fw 190 very tightly around the latest 14-cylinder BMW 139 radial engine; he had been much impressed by Pratt & Whitney radials from the USA. The prototype flew on 1 June 1939 with Flugkapitän Hans Sander at the controls. It boasted excellent handling, good visibility and a high top speed (389 mph). It rolled easily and, with a wide, inwardly retracting undercarriage, was stable on take-off and landing. Its cockpit was a small masterpiece of modern, ergonomic design; the pilot was assisted by electrically operated flaps and landing gear. The stall speed of the Fw 190, though, was 127 mph compared to the Bf 109's impressively slow 75 mph. This was, in every sense, a fast aeroplane. Deliveries of Fw 190A-1s, with BMW 801 engines, to frontline combat units were made in August and September 1941, although overheating engines proved a worrying problem for Tank and, indeed, the whole 190 production programme, until their replacement by the new BMW 801C-2 motor in the spring of 1942.

The new fighter had a top speed of 408 mph. It was well armed with two 7.92-mm machine-guns firing through the propeller, together with one from each wing root, and a pair of wing-mounted 20-mm cannon. Fw 190A-5s fitted with bomb racks for one 1,100-lb bomb under the fuselage and a 550-lb bomb under each wing became a disturbingly familiar sight over England in 1942 and 1943 when they were used to strike strategic targets as well as for nuisance raids. As the war went on, the Fw 190, like the Bf 109, was used in increasingly varied roles. To keep pace with the Griffon-engined Spitfire Mk XIV and P-51D Mustang, the long-nosed Fw 190D appeared in 1944, powered by a supercharged Jumo 213A liquid-cooled V12. When boosted, this engine could produce a temporary maximum of 2,050 hp; the Fw 190D had a top speed of 440 mph at 37,000 feet. The radial-engined 190 continued in production in plants spread across Poland and increasingly staffed with forced labour, with tank-busting variants such as the heavily armour-plated 190F-8, armed with fourteen rockets as well as cannon and machine-guns. There was even a torpedo-carrying variant.

The Fw 190D was produced in limited numbers, yet it was a close competitor to the Mk XIV Spitfire. Both aircraft had engines of similar power and their maximum speed was much the same. The Spitfire could turn inside the Focke-Wulf, but the German machine rolled faster. Too little and too late, the Ta 152H high-altitude evolution of the 190 appeared in the autumn of 1944; after only thirty-one hours of test-flying, production began in earnest in

November. A mere sixty-seven of these exceptional aircraft were built, with just two being operational on 30 April 1945. They had been, nevertheless, highly promising, faster, at 472 mph, and more manoeuvrable than both the American P-51D Mustang and P-47 Thunderbolt. Tank himself flew one and was able to escape from a posse of Mustangs by applying full power and full boost into a dive. The Ta 152's lower-flying cousin, the Fw 190D, meanwhile, worked hard to protect airfields used by Messerschmitt Me 262 jets from Allied fighters. Other 190s were equipped in the very last days of the German war to fly unmanned Ju 88 Mistel bombers by remote control. No one could accuse Tank and his colleagues of a lack of ingenuity. In all, 13,376 Fw 190s had been built in six Focke-Wulf plants, and also by Arado, Ago and Fieseler.

Oberleutnant Otto Kittel was the top-scoring Fw 190 ace. He had first flown Bf 109s on the Eastern Front in autumn 1941. In early 1943, and with fifteen victories under his wings, he moved on to Fw 190s. When he was shot down near Dzukste, Latvia, by Soviet Il-2 Shturmoviks on 16 February 1945 and killed, twenty-seven-year-old Kittel's score was 267 kills. Several other air forces flew Tank's fighter. The Hungarian Air Force fielded seventy Fw 190s during the war. The Turkish Air Force flew a total of seventy, alongside Spitfires, until 1949. The French Armée de l'Air flew sixty-five brand-new Fw 190s manufactured in 1945–6 by the Société Nationale de Construction Aéronautique at Cravant, a former Luftwaffe repair base. The last flew in June 1949. Otherwise, a solitary Fw 190 made its way to Japan for design analysis during the war. One was used for pilot training in Poland after the war, while another solo Fw 190 was preserved by the Yugoslav Air Force, having been captured by partisans and flown in anger against its former masters.

Tank himself slipped away with a number of Focke-Wulf personnel to Argentina at the end of the war. As Professor Dr Pedro Matthies, he worked at the government's Instituto Aerotecnic, Cordoba. He very nearly saw a new aircraft into production, the IAe Pulqui II, based on designs for an Fw Ta 183 prototype of 1945, but with the fall of his patron, President Juan Peron, in 1955, the Focke-Wulf team broke up. Some went to the USA, while Tank journeyed to India, where he designed that country's first indigenous military aircraft, the beautiful Hindustan Marut subsonic jet fighter, which served in the IAF from 1961 to 1985, when it was replaced by Soviet MiGs. Tank returned to Berlin in the 1970s.

The Fw 190 had been one nasty surprise for Spitfire pilots. The Me 262 was something else again: a jet fighter heralding a new age that would make the piston-engined fighter redundant. Although British Gloster Meteor jets did see service with the RAF from August 1944 onwards, they were much slower than the German aircraft and not used in combat against the Luftwaffe. As usual, it was up to Spitfire pilots to tackle the new jet menace.

First flown by Fritz Wendel on 18 July 1942 in Leipheim, Germany, the swept-wing Messerschmitt Me 262 Schwalbe (Swallow), or 'Turbo' as it was called by Luftwaffe pilots, was the world's first operational turbojet aircraft. Bizarrely, given its impressive performance, production was delayed until late 1943 and even then Hitler insisted that the aircraft be used primarily as a fighter-bomber rather than as an interceptor. Fortunately for the Allies, the Me 262 came too late to turn the tide of war. Although more than 1,400 were built, fewer than 300 saw combat. A lack of fuel, spare parts, materials such as tungsten and chrome, and trained pilots were also factors holding this fighter of the future at bay, as were jamming cannons and a tendency for early production aircraft to break up in flight. Although highly effective in the air, and devastatingly fast by the standards of the time, the heavy Me 262, like all early jets, was slow to take off and land, and therefore vulnerable. Its airfields had to be protected by fighters, mainly Fw 190Ds, that might have been employed in action elsewhere. Me 262s destroyed approximately 150 Allied aircraft for losses of about 100. The situation might well have been very different if the German jet had been put into active service a year earlier. As it was, in September 1944, General Carl Spaatz, comm- ander of US Strategic Air Forces Europe, suggested that if greater numbers of German jets were on the way, the cancellation of the Allied daylight bombing offensive might be a real possibility.

To show just how effective the German jets could be, on 18 March 1945, thirty-seven Me 262s intercepted an aerial fleet of no fewer than 1,221 Allied bombers, escorted by 632 fighters. The Me 262s shot down twelve bombers and one fighter for the loss of three of their own. Many were flown under the command of General Adolf Galland, whose first kill in the Second World War was a Hurricane as he flew a Bf 109E during the Battle of France in 1940, and whose last was a USAAF B-26 Marauder bomber as he flew an Me 262 on 26 April 1945. If the Me 262s could have maintained the ratio of destruction they had achieved on 18 March 1945 for months on end, the Allied air forces might have been in trouble. But time was very much against the German jet.

The first Me 262 flew in combat on 25 July 1944, surprising the crew of a normally invulnerable Mosquito on reconnaissance duty. Armed with four 30-mm cannon and twenty-four R4M rockets, the single-seat Me 262 was powered by a pair of underwing- mounted Junkers Jumo 004 engines producing a combined thrust of 3,960 lbs. This gave the jet a top speed of 540 mph and a ceiling of 38,000 feet. Its range was 650 miles. The two principal Luftwaffe versions were the Me 262A-1A Schwalbe interceptor, and the Me 262A-2A Sturmvogel (Storm Bird) fighter-bomber, which could carry a bomb load of 1,100 lbs.

Willy Messerschmitt had begun development of his jet fighter in 1938, just two years after K5054 made its maiden flight from Eastleigh, and a full set of plans was drawn up by April 1939. However, as Albert Speer later explained, there was little interest among the top echelons of German government: Hitler and Goering dismissed such weapons as the Me 262 and V1 because this was a new technology they did not understand and they failed to grasp its importance until very late in the Nazi day. The prototype flew with a Junkers Jumo 210 engine driving a propeller, so that the airframe could be tested while BMW 003 turbojets were being readied. This was just as well, as the first Me 262 to fly with these powerplants suffered a failure in both, and was only able to land safely because the Jumo and propeller were there to help. The BMW engines were replaced by the Jumo 004. Even though this was to prove less reliable than the Rolls-Royce Welland installed in the RAF's first frontline jet, the Gloster Meteor, the British aircraft's top speed was some 125mph less than its German rival's.

The sheer speed of the Me 262 made it a difficult opponent for Allied fighter pilots. However, because it was less manoeuvrable than Spitfires and Mustangs, it could be caught while turning if the piston-engined fighters were in a very fast dive. To boost speed, even if only for a few moments, the Americans began injecting nitrous oxide into the Merlin engines of Mustangs. This is the same gas used to give dragsters their sensational off-the-line acceleration. Most of the Me 262s destroyed by Allied fighters were on the ground. Reports of successful air-to-air combat involving Spitfires are rare, but they do exist.

On the evening of 14 February 1945, Flight Lieutenant F. A. O. Gaze of RAF 610 Squadron was flying a Mk XIV on patrol over Nijmegen, Holland. After a failed attempt to attack an Arado 234 twin-engined reconnaissance jet, Gaze reported: 'Then I did an orbit at 13,000 feet to clear off the ice on the windscreen and sighted three Me 262s in Vic formation passing below me at cloud-top level. I dived down behind them and closed in, crossing behind the formation, and attacked the port aircraft, which was lagging slightly. I could not see my sight properly as we were flying straight into the sun, but fired from dead astern, at a range of 350 yards, hitting it in the starboard jet with the second burst; at which the other two aircraft immediately dived into cloud. It pulled up slowly and turned to starboard and I fired, obtaining more strikes on fuselage and jet which caught fire. The enemy rolled over on to its back and dived through cloud. I turned 180 and dived after it, calling on the R/T to warn my No. 2; on breaking cloud I saw an aircraft hit the ground and explode about a mile ahead of me... I claim this Me 262 destroyed. Black 2 [Gaze's No. 2] also witnessed this explosion.'

On 13 March 1945, Flying Officer Howard C. Nicholson of RCAF 402 Squadron was also flying a Mk XIV: 'I was flying Yellow 3 on a fighter sweep in the Gladback [München Gladbach] area when I sighted an Me 262 at about 5,000 feet flying South-West. He did not appear to see me. I broke and fired a three-second burst from 250 yards line astern into his starboard wing and the base of the fuselage. Smoke poured out and pieces flew off the starboard wing. I kept firing, observing many hits, and the aircraft tended to fall out of control, regaining slowly. At 2,000 feet he went into a sharp dive to port but owing to the extremely heavy flak from Gladback, I broke to starboard. I did not see him crash, but this is confirmed by the C.O. of 402 Squadron. I claim one Me 262 destroyed.'

Although the Spitfire was no match for the Me 262 in terms of speed and high-speed climb, its wing was, again, to prove superior to that of even this ultra-modern rival. Tests demonstrated that the Me 262 would fly out of control at a speed in excess of Mach 0.86, and that its airframe was in danger of breaking up at a marginally higher speed. The Spitfire had bettered this in 1943. Although Messerschmitt prepared three fascinating Hochgeschwindigkeit, or high-speed, Me 262 variants in 1944–5, none was tested at above Mach 0.86.

Post-war, Me 262s and their pilots were closely examined and cross-examined by the Allies and Soviets. Meanwhile, Czechoslovak-built Me 262 variants continued in production for a number of years, with single- (Avia S-92) and twin-seat (Avia CS-92) versions of the jet flying until 1957. Five upgraded replica Me 262s have been built in the United States, the first flying, successfully, in January 2003.

By 1943, the war was finally going against Germany. Although aircraft production in the Reich was to reach an astonishing all-time high during 1944, it became clear that Hitler needed new weapons to hold back the Allies. Indeed, Winston Churchill had been sent the following memorandum from General Sir Hastings Ismay, Deputy Secretary (military) to the War Cabinet: 'The Chief-of-Staff feels that you should be made aware of reports of German experiments with long-range rockets. The fact that five reports have been received since the end of 1942 indicates a foundation of fact even if details are inaccurate...no time should be lost in establishing the facts and in devising counter-measures...It is not considered desirable to inform the public at this stage, when the evidence is so intangible.' Then, at the first light of dawn on 13 June 1944, a week after D-Day, the specially formed German 155th Flakregiment launched the first FZG-76, or V1, flying bomb against London. It fell on the village of Swanscombe, Kent. Nine others followed that morning. Four crashed on take-off, two fell into the Channel and three got through. Six civilians were killed by the V1 that struck the railway bridge over Grove Road in east London's Mile End.

Two days later, 244 V1s were launched from fifty-five sites. Of these, seventy-three hit the Greater London area and seventy-one fell outside it. Hitler was thrilled. On 17 June, he flew to northern France to congratulate the V1 team and to see the rockets in action for himself. On 18 June, the anniversary of the Battle of Waterloo and of Churchill's 'finest hour' speech of 1940, 500 V1s were launched. One of those falling on London hit the Guards Chapel at Wellington Barracks, St James's, killing 121 people and wounding sixty-eight more. It was the beginning of a new Blitz.

The V stood for 'Vergeltungswaffen': vengeance or reprisal weapon. The British knew the two-ton rocket as the 'doodlebug' or 'buzz bomb'. Twenty-six feet long and with a wingspan of seventeen feet, the V1 was powered by a pulse-jet engine and carried a 1,870-lb explosive warhead. It could be launched, with a hefty shove from a steam-powered catapult, from rails laid on camouflaged concrete ramps in Holland, the Pas de Calais and the Somme-Seine and Cherbourg areas, or from under the wings of suitably modified Heinkel He 111 bombers. Either way, it had a range of 150 miles, later extended to 250 miles, and flew at anywhere between 300 and 4,500 feet, with a blazing exhaust, at up to 400 mph. A simple gyroscopic compass kept it on track.

British intelligence had been well aware of the threat. On 17 August 1943, Bomber Command flew a massive raid against the top-secret Nazi rocket research and production plant at Peenemunde on the Baltic coast, killing scientists and slave labourers alike. The Germans moved their operation to the Harz mountains, out of reach of Allied bombers, while test flights were made in Poland. Between January and June 1944, the RAF flew Spitfire and Hurricane sorties against V1 launch pads, but the damage they caused was quickly repaired.

One way of knocking out the V1s was to attack them using fighters. These needed to be exceptionally fast at low levels to catch and destroy 'doodlebugs'. The Spitfire Mk XIV was fast enough, as was the Mk IX – at a push – together with the Hawker Tempest V, De Havilland Mosquito, P-51D Mustang and P-47M Thunderbolt. The new Gloster Meteor jets were certainly fast enough to catch V1s, but problems with jamming cannons meant they shot down just thirteen. The fighters, though, had to carry out their task in the nail-biting interim it took V1s to fly between the 1,600 anti-aircraft guns that were set up along the coast by mid-July, each firing an average of 2,500 shells for each V1 destroyed, and the thousand barrage balloons helping to protect London, or else had to attack them while they were still over the Channel.

Fighter pilots discovered that, short of successfully shooting down a V1, which was not a good idea over built-up areas, there were two ways to knock the flying bombs out of the sky. One was to fly a Spitfire's wing just six inches below the V1's; the resulting disturbance to the airflow would often, though not always, tip the flying bomb's wing up, upset its gyros and send it into an uncontrolled dive. The other was to tip the rocket off balance with a fighter's wing. Machine-guns had little impact on the steel airframes of V1s, which, in any case, had few vulnerable moving parts, while 20-mm cannon shells could cause the flying bomb to explode and probably destroy the attacking fighter in the process.

RAF fighters did a good job bringing down an average of thirty V1s a day, with anti-aircraft guns accounting for a further ten; this meant that about sixty V1s a day still got through to their loosely defined target. The last V1 struck British soil on 29 March 1945. In the final reckoning, 6,725 V1s were recorded flying towards or over London, and a total of 9,251 over England. Between them, fighters and A-A guns, now radar-directed thanks to the latest US technology, destroyed very nearly 3,500. Central London was hit by 2,340, which killed 5,475 people and injured at least 16,000. The weapon was later used, with devastating effect, against the Belgian port of Antwerp.

The Fi 103 V1 was designed by Fritz Gosslau of the Argus engine works and Robert Lusser of the Gerhard Fieseler Werke, an aircraft factory founded by the First World War fighter ace and aerobatic champion in 1930. Fieseler was feted for its highly successful sailplanes and sports aircraft, and particularly for its insect-like Fi 156 Storch, an observation aircraft able to take off and land on little more than a silver Reichsmark and of which some 2,500 examples were built. During the early stages of the war, Fieseler produced Bf 109 and Fw 190 fighters. In late 1941, Fieseler's V1 or 'aerial torpedo' made its maiden flight at Peenemunde, powered by an Argus As 14 pulse jet, first developed in 1934, producing a thrust of 660 lbs. It was the pulsing explosions of fuel inside the motor that gave the V1 its characteristic sound. Although initially seeming like something from a 1930s science-fiction film, the V1 was a fairly simple device, and with a fuselage made of sheet metal it was easy to make: one for every fifty man hours of labour.

To hit long-range targets, including Manchester, V1s were launched from He 111s over the North Sea. At the very end of the war, a number of piloted suicide V1s, known as Reichenbergs, were to have been launched in this manner, while others would have been towed by Arado Ar 234 jet bombers. Fortunately, hostilities ended before such drastic plans could be put into action. By this time, somewhere between 30,000 and 35,000 V1s had been produced. After the war, variations of the V1 were made for a brief period in France, the Soviet Union and the United States.

As for the Italians, R. J. Mitchell had seen just how good their aircraft design could be during the later years of the Schneider Trophy when his Supermarine floatplanes raced against Mussolini's best. By the time of the Battle of Britain, however, when Mitchell's Spitfires took on Italian warplanes for the first time, it was hardly a contest. The Italian aircraft involved were antiquated. They were a joy to fly, but no match for the latest generation of British eight-gun, V12-engined monoplane fighters. Although dating from the late 1930s, and still very much in production, machines such as the Fiat CR 42 biplane and the Fiat G 50bis monoplane, both flown by the Regia Aeronautica's Corpo Aereo Italiano, based in Belgium under the command of General Rino Corso-Fougier from October 1940 to April 1941, looked as if they were throwbacks to another age. They had little success in action. The G 50s had such a short range that they saw very little combat, while the CR 42s were almost sitting ducks for the RAF's finest.

164

Morale among Italian pilots was understandably low. Sergente Pietro Salvadori of 95a Squadriglia made a forced landing in a CR 42 near the lighthouse at Orford Ness, Suffolk. Salvadori told his captors that he did not want to fight any more, that he did not like the weather in Belgium, or Belgian food, or his German colleagues. Few Italian fighters were equipped with radios, while a lack of heaters meant that pilots were prey to frostbite. Salvadori's aircraft, MM5071, now preserved at the RAF Museum in Hendon, was test flown by Captain Eric M. Brown, RN. He found the Fiat a delight to fly. It was fast for a biplane, with a top speed of 270 mph, and gloriously aerobatic; it was also poorly protected, lightly armed and generally vulnerable to attack. It did indeed seem odd that a country which had produced some of the world's finest seaplanes, sports and racing cars in the 1930s, as well as much advanced structural engineering, should have lagged so far behind the British and Germans in the design and manufacture of military aircraft.

When, however, Spitfire pilots next encountered Italian veterans of the Battle of Britain, over Malta, things were rather different. The MC 202 Folgore (Lightning), designed by Mario Castoldi, chief engineer of Aeronautica Macchi, was first flown on 10 August 1940, and was a Bf 109-like single-seat monoplane fighter powered by either a 1,175-hp Daimler-Benz DB601 or, later, an equally powerful Alfa Romeo RA 1000 RC 41 fuel-injected Monsone (Monsoon) V12 engine. Entering service the following year, the MC 202 was, despite an airframe based on an earlier Castoldi design, the MC 200, a vast improvement on existing Italian fighters. It was widely considered superior to both the Hawker Hurricane and Curtiss P-40 Kittyhawks it fought against, at first on the Libyan front from November 1941, and the equal of the Mk V Spitfire. It was able to out-turn all three, although the Spitfire had a superior rate of climb. The Folgore had a top speed of 372 mph at 18,370 feet, a ceiling of 37,730 feet and was armed with two 12.7-mm Breda-SAFAT machine-guns firing through the propeller and two 7.7-mm machine-guns mounted in the wings. By late 1942, it was the most numerous Italian fighter and approximately 1,500 were built. There were few variations.

The pilots of the Regia Aeronautica loved their Lightnings. Performance was strong and controls were light, well-balanced and responsive. Despite the hefty turning power of their V12 engines, MC 202s did not veer to one side under acceleration on take-off because, ingeniously, their left wings were twenty-one centimetres longer than their right wings: the longer wing generated more lift and so counteracted what would have been the aircraft's normal tendency to turn to the left. Nothing less should have been expected of a design by Dr Mario Castoldi. He had been R. J. Mitchell's great rival in the later Schneider Trophy races. His beautiful MC 72 racer of 1931 was, in the event, beaten by engine troubles, but on 23 October 1934 it captured the world speed record for seaplanes at 440.68 mph, a record that stood for very nearly the next fifty years.

The Folgore fought over North Africa and Malta and against Allied convoys in the Mediterranean, in defence of Sicily and southern Italy and, in lesser numbers, on the Eastern Front. It was superseded by the Macchi MC 205 Veltro (Greyhound), a tougher, faster and altogether more furious version of the MC 202.

With a top speed of some 400 mph and equipped, eventually, with a pair of 20-mm Breda cannon as well as 12.7-mm machine-guns, the MC 205 was much respected by Allied and Luftwaffe

A line-up of Italian Macchi MC 202s in 1942.

pilots alike, but entered the war in June 1943, far too late to stave off defeat. Powered by a Fiat version of the 1,475-hp Daimler-Benz DB 605 engine known as the Tifone (Typhoon), the Greyhound was a great, if very limited, success. By the time of the Italian surrender on 3 September 1943, there were just sixty-six in service, of which only thirty-five were airworthy. Six of these went on to serve with the Allies as part of the Aeronautica Cobelligerante de Sud, while twenty-nine were flown north to join the ranks of the Axis-aligned Aviazione della RSI (Repubblica Sociale Italiana), which continued to fight alongside the Luftwaffe on behalf of Mussolini's last-ditch Repubblica di Salò. Production of the MC 205 continued at the Macchi factory at Varese, north of Milan, until this was destroyed by Allied bombing. Just 262

Veltros had been completed, some of them going into service, mostly in the Balkans, with the Luftwaffe.

In action, they had proved to be extremely effective. On 9 July 1943, six Sicilian-based MC 205s intercepted a group of twenty twin-engined USAAF P-38 Lockheed Lightnings and RAF P-40 Kittyhawks. Six Allied aircraft were lost to one Italian. While Sicilian Veltro squadrons flew up to six missions a day, Macchi itself was currently only able to build an average of 1.5 new fighters a day. Not only were supplies of just about everything required for their production in extremely short supply, but, like the Spitfire, the Veltro was tricky, and thus slow, to build. The Veltros that flew for the Republic of Salò destroyed a large number of Allied bombers and successfully tackled the formidable P-51D Mustang.

Italy's top-scoring ace, the highly decorated Adriano Visconti, achieved eleven of his twenty-six victories in the few weeks he was able to fly a Veltro. He later flew Bf 109Gs, but was executed by Italian partisans after being shot down. Italy's number two ace, Teresio Martinoli, claimed two Spitfires while flying MC 205s with the Regia Aeronautica. After the war, forty-two MC 205s, almost all of them converted 202s, were sold to the Royal Egyptian Air Force and flew alongside Spitfire Mk IXs. On 7 January 1949, one destroyed an Israeli P-51D Mustang.

On the other side of the world, the Japanese aero industry was geared up to the production of tactical fighters – machines that would fly a supporting role in the air forces of the Imperial Army and Navy. Japanese fighters of the late 1930s were lightweight machines, designed to fly beautifully and over long distances, especially across water, but they were under-armed and innocent of armour-plating. Light, lithe and highly manoeuvrable, the long-ranged Mitsubishi A6M Zero fighter fought with the Imperial Japanese Navy throughout the war in the Far East from the attack on the US fleet at Pearl Harbor, Hawaii, on 7 December 1941 to the last desperate sorties against B-29s raining bombs on Japanese cities in August 1945. It was the world's first shipboard fighter capable of tackling its land-based opponents with real authority. It was a deadly foe in dogfights, much loved by those who flew it, rightly feared by those who fought it. Although ultimately overtaken by Allied fighter development, the Zero was built by Mitsubishi and Nakajima until the very end of the Second World War, when 10,931 (although figures vary) had been completed.

The final design brief for the new carrier-based fighter had been issued by the Imperial Navy to both the Nakajima and Mitsubishi works in October 1937. This called for a maximum speed of 310 mph at 13,100 feet, an ability to climb to 9,800 feet in 3.5 minutes, and an endurance of up to two hours. The fighter was to be armed with two 20-mm cannon and two 12.7-mm machine-guns. Curiously, given their later success with high-speed fighters, Nakajima pulled out in November 1938, leaving the field clear for Mitsubishi's design team at Nagoya led by Jiro Horikoshi. His solution was a low-winged, light-alloy monoplane with the pilot sitting under a distinctive glass-house that offered all-round visibility. The aircraft was powered by a compact Mitsubishi Zuisei 13 (Auspicious Star), 14-cylinder, air-cooled radial engine developing a maximum of 875 hp at 11,810 feet and driving a two-bladed, variable-pitch propeller. The A6M1's maiden flight was made by the test pilot Katsuzo Shima at Kagamigahara on 1 April 1939. The aircraft had been towed to the airfield in an ox-cart. Aside from the fitting of a new three-bladed propeller, little work needed to be done before the Navy took delivery of the aircraft at the end of October.

The test aircraft weighed just 4,380 lbs compared to the Spitfire prototype's 5,332 lbs; it could easily out-turn Mitchell's marvel. The A6M1, however, was not quite fast enough for the Navy, which ordered Mitsubishi to replace the Zuisei engine with the 950-hp Nakajima NK1C Sakae 12 (Prosperity) 14-cylinder radial powerplant. The potent new fighter, now designated A6M2, entered service in July 1940. Because the Navy listed the A6M2 as its Type O Carrier Fighter, a reference to the Japanese year 2600 (1940), it quickly became known as the Reisen, an abbreviation of Rei Shiki Sento Ki, or 2600. The Allies, who attached codenames to all Japanese aircraft, knew the A6M as the Zeke, although, in fact, nearly everyone and all sides knew it as the Reisen or Zero.

The Zero scored its first air-to-air victories on 13 September 1940, when thirteen A6M2s led by Lieutenant Saburo Shindo attacked twenty-seven Soviet-built Polikarpov I-15 and I-16 fighters of the Chinese Nationalist Air Force. For no losses, the Zero pilots wiped out the entire Chinese contingent. And so it continued. Before they were redeployed a year later, the Zeros had shot down ninety-nine Chinese aircraft for the loss of only two of their number, and these to ground fire.

During December 1941 and the first months of 1942, as the Japanese won victory after victory in South-East Asia and the Pacific, the Zero took on all comers with confident ease. The American Grumman F4F Wildcat and Bell P-39 Airacobra were no match for the A6M, although the freelance Flying Tiger squadrons, later incorporated within the USAAF, achieved some degree of success with their shark-mouthed Curtiss P-40s. But first they had had to learn that the only way to take on a

A restored Japanese Mitsubishi A6M3 Model 22 Zero.

marauding Zero was to dive at it from above, make a brief firing pass and then beat a hasty retreat. For the Allies, the breakthrough was to come in July 1942 on the remote Aleutian island of Akutau, where a Zero pilot had crash-landed and died. Five weeks later, US troops found the aircraft, with the body of its pilot still hanging upside down from the straps, and shipped it back to San Diego, California. The Zero's superb handling was now fully recognized. Orders were issued to pilots not to engage with the Zero in dogfights, especially at low altitude, but to dive, strike and dive again, just as the Flying Tigers had been doing.

The Zero was developed throughout the war, gradually increasing in power and putting on weight, some of it in the form of much-needed armour. It had been designed initially as a pure attacker, and so little thought was given to protecting the pilot or fuel tanks. The most numerous and widely built model was the

A6M5, but this ultimately proved to be little competition for such tough and capable new US aircraft as the Grumman F6F Hellcat and Vought F4U Corsair.

The only RAF fighters Zero pilots normally encountered were P-40s and Hurricanes. Later, Zeros did occasionally meet Mk VIII Spitfires, especially over Burma. As long as Spitfire pilots stuck to the Flying Tigers' rules – no low and slow dogfighting – they had little to fear. By this time, though, the Zero was no longer the scourge it had once been. Its intended successor, the altogether heavier, larger and faster Mitsubishi A7M Reppu (Hurricane) or Sam, also designed by Jiro Horikoshi, was far too late to save the day for the Japanese; by the end of the war, just one production aircraft had been completed.

The precise scores of the leading Japanese aces are still disputed. Like all fighter pilots, they were prone to making inflated claims, and the extant records are sparse. Yet theirs was also a culture that discouraged the elevation of the individual over the group, and so victories were often credited to units rather than particular pilots. Nonetheless, the man who is generally considered to have been Japan's ace of aces, the taciturn Hiroyoshi Nishizawa, flew the Zero – as did his main rival for the title, Tetsuzo Iwamoto. Some sources put Nishizawa's tally in the eighties; others think it was higher. What is certain, though, is that Nishizawa did not survive the war: he was killed when a bomber ferrying him and a group of fellow pilots to collect replacement Zeros was shot down over the Philippines in October 1944.

The Zero is, of course, the best-known Japanese fighter of the conflict, although in terms of numbers of enemy aircraft destroyed the Nakajima Ki-43 Hayabusa (Peregrine Falcon) was more successful. Known to the Allies as the Oscar, the Ki-43 was a tactical fighter that flew with the Imperial Japanese Army wherever it fought: China, Burma, the Malay Peninsula, New Guinea, the Philippines, countless South Pacific islands and the Japanese home islands. Designed by a team led by Nakajima's Hideo Itokawa, the future rocket scientist, and first flown in January 1939, the Ki-43 was an unknown quantity when first encountered by Allied pilots. Like the Zero, which it resembled, the radial-engined Oscar was light, manoeuvrable and easy to fly. Total production amounted to 5,919 aircraft but, with its lightweight construction, lack of armour until late in the day, and its limited firepower from just two 12.7-mm machine-guns, the Ki-43 proved no match for the Allied fighters it met during the later years of the war. Nevertheless, the Oscar shot down more Allied aircraft than any other Japanese fighter. It was a simple and nippy machine – with a top speed of between 330 and 360 mph, an excellent view from the cockpit and a range of up to 1,990 miles with drop-tanks – and the Ki-43 was even to serve with both the Indonesians against the Dutch and the French against the Vietnamese after the war.

The air force of the Imperial Army fielded an altogether heavier and more powerful fighter in the Kawasaki Ki-61 Hien (Swallow). In 1937, Kawasaki had bought a Daimler-Benz 601 engine, from which it developed its own, copycat 1,175-hp Ha-40. Completed in December 1941, the prototype Hien, which had a top speed of 368 mph, was pitted against a captured P-40E Warhawk and a Bf 109E that had been shipped to Japan by submarine. The results were impressive, and the new and only liquid-cooled Japanese fighter, known to the Allies as Tony, went into action over and around New Guinea in April 1943. Because, unlike every other Japanese fighter, the Ki-61 was designed first and foremost for sheer speed and power, and because of its profile, it was mistaken by Allied pilots for a German or, if not that, an Italian aircraft – which is why it was called Antonio, or Tony for short.

Improved and more heavily armed versions followed in 1944 and 1945, but these arrived too late to threaten Allied fighters. The engines were also often unreliable. When the Akashi engine plant manufacturing the Ha-140 engine was destroyed by B-29 bombers in January 1945, Ki-61 airframes were adapted to take Mitsubishi's Ha-112-II 14-cylinder radial engine producing 1,500 hp. The result, the Ki-100, a Japanese Fw 190, proved to be a superb fighter, more than capable of tackling Hellcats and Corsairs as well as Mustangs and P-47N Thunderbolts and the huge and high-flying B-29 Superfortress bombers they escorted.

But it was the robust and capable Nakajima Ki-84 Hayate (Gale) that was generally considered to be the finest Japanese fighter of the Second World War. It did, though, have its problems. One was increasingly poor production quality as the war went on, with the result that one aircraft might perform a lot better, or worse, than another from the same factory. The other was its storming but unreliable 1,990-hp Ha-45 18-cylinder direct-injection radial engine. On form, though, the Ki-84 was both fast – able to out-climb both the P-51D and the P-47N – and chuckable in the hands of expert pilots. It was also well armed, the Ki-84-Ib having two 20-mm wing-mounted cannon and two more firing through the propeller. In the event, just 3,514 appear to have been built.

Designed by Nakajima's project engineer T. Koyama, the prototype Ki-84 was completed at the Ota plant, Gumma Prefecture, in March 1943. It flew the following month. The fourth prototype reached 394 mph at 21,800 feet and 496 mph in a dive. The Ki-84 was first flown into action against the Americans in August 1944. Codenamed Frank by Colonel Frank McCoy of the Allied Technical Air Intelligence Unit, this Japanese Army Air Force fighter could out-turn a Spitfire and out-climb even the high-performance P-51H model Mustang. Allied bombing of Japanese aircraft factories effectively put paid to the production of the Ki-84 and, of course, to its development, which still had some way to go before it could be truly said to have been as good a fighter as the Mustang or Spitfire.

The Japanese deployed other fighters of note. The Japanese Army Air Force's Nakajima Ki-44 Shoki (Devil Queller) or Tojo, after Japan's wartime prime minister, and the Navy's Mitsubishi J2M Raiden (Thunderbolt) or Jack were purpose-built interceptors whose design, much to the initial dismay of those who flew them, sacrificed manoeuvrability for speed and rate of climb. Neither type was built in great numbers – 1,225 Ki-44s and some 480 J2Ms – but both proved to be effective bomber destroyers and eventually won the grudging respect of their pilots. And although the Zero was never really superseded, there was one Imperial Navy fighter which could, perhaps, have legitimately claimed to be its spiritual successor. This was the Kawanishi N1K1-J and N1K2-J Shiden (Violet Lightning) or George. Unusually derived from a floatplane fighter, the N1K1 Kyofu (Mighty Wind) or Rex, the well-armed Shiden entered service in early 1944. Its two variants combined sparkling performance with excellent manoeuvrability. Some 1,430 were built, and in the hands of a capable pilot the type proved a real threat to American Hellcats and Corsairs. But it was hobbled by the unreliability of its mighty Homare (Honour) powerplant, and further development of the Shiden was simply overtaken by events.

The Zero may have trounced its Russian-built opposition over China in 1940–41, but the Soviet aero industry had nonetheless achieved much in the previous decade. There had, for example, been a remarkable opening up of the Russian Far East with an assortment of impressive multi-engined machines carrying explorers vast distances across bitterly cold Arctic landscapes. And in the tiny, barrel-shaped Polikarpov I-16, the Soviets could claim to have introduced into service the world's first low-wing monoplane fighter with a retractable undercarriage. But when Hitler launched Operation Barbarossa, the German invasion of Russia, in June 1941, the VVS was ill-equipped to fight back, possessing no fighter capable of taking on the Bf 109 or, later, the Fw 190: the I-16 was by now plainly obsolete, and the more modern MiG-3 and LaGG-3 were simply inadequate. Besides, Stalin had wiped out so many officers during his purges of the late 1930s that, like the other armed services, the VVS lacked both skilled pilots and experienced commanders. In the opening days, weeks and months of Barbarossa, the VVS suffered horrendous losses, but the terrible Russian winter was to save the Soviet Union. While the Allies supplied the likes of Hurricanes and Spitfires, P-40s and P-39s to help in the interim, Soviet factories, now relocated well away from the Germans to the east of the Ural mountains, began to build machines that could fight their own war.

For years I must have looked at a little red Soviet postage stamp mounted in my childhood album without knowing the identity of the aircraft busy shooting down a fighter with a swastika on its tail. The stamp turns out to have been issued to coincide with Soviet Air Force Day, 1945; the powerful-looking fighter it depicts, in red, of course, was a Lavochkin La-7, the finest Russian fighter of the Second World War, and yet an aircraft much overlooked, or simply unknown, elsewhere in the world. Many people outside the former USSR are familiar with the prefixes Yak and MiG, but La?

La-7 pilots took on Focke-Wulf 190s, both on stamps and in the air, and even had a crack at the Messerschmitt 262 with a confidence that would have been all but impossible before these fast and nimble fighters made their aerial debut in the summer of 1944. The Soviet Union's leading air ace of what in Russia is known as the Great Patriotic War achieved many of his sixty-two victories behind the gunsight of an La-7. He was the Ukrainian-born Ivan Nikitovich Kozhedub, nicknamed 'Ivan the Terrible', a three-time hero of the Soviet Union who went on to fly MiG-15 jets in the Korean War and rose to the rank of air marshal. He scored his last seventeen victories in 1945 in the La-7 numbered 27, which is now preserved in the sprawling, and utterly compelling, Monino State Aviation Museum on the outskirts of Moscow.

The La-7, rightly feared by Luftwaffe pilots, was a development of a sequence of largely timber-built fighter aircraft beginning with the liquid-cooled LaGG-1 of 1938, designed for the VVS by Semyon Alekseyevich Lavochkin. The wartime production version of the LaGG-1, the LaGG-3, was built in large numbers but remained far from satisfactory in terms of both performance and build quality. Playing on the name 'Lag', VVS pilots knew the LaGG-3 as the 'varnished guaranteed coffin' (*lakirovanny garantirovanny grob*). Everything changed, and very much for the better, when Lavochkin turned to a new and powerful air-cooled radial engine. The resulting La-5 was the best Soviet fighter to date. With metal alloys available in reasonable quantities from 1943 onwards, Lavochkin began rapid work on the development of the La-5. The prototype, lighter and more powerful than its predecessor, flew in November 1943 and was put into mass production almost immediately in factories located in Moscow and in the Yaroslavl region. Lavochkin was awarded a Stalin Prize of 100,000 roubles for the design of the ensuing La-7. Both he and his aircraft had come a long way in five hectic years.

The first production La-7 entered service with the 176th Guards Fighter Aviation Regiment in July 1944. The La-7 was 44 mph faster than the Fw 190 and could both out-climb and out-turn its German rival. Now, at last, VVS pilots had a weapon that could more than meet the Germans on their own terms. They sorely needed a fighter as competent as the La-7; the VVS was to lose a staggering 77,000 military aircraft, and perhaps as many as 83,000, between June 1941 and May 1945. Many regiments were keen to swap their liquid-cooled Yaks for La-7s, as the air-cooled aircraft were not only generally superior in flight, but also better able to withstand the extremes of heat and cold common in the Russian summer and winter.

The La-7 weighed 7,480 lbs all up and, powered by a Shvetsov ASh-82FN engine rated at a maximum of 1,850 hp, it climbed well – at 3,608 feet per minute – and had a top speed of 425 mph. Armed with two or three ShVAK 20-mm cannon, its greatest weapon, speed aside, was its ability to turn quickly and very tightly. The fighter flew in service with the VVS into 1947; it also served with the North Korean, Czechoslovakian and Romanian Air Forces. Experimental versions of the La-7 were built with a variety of jet and rocket motors, although none was considered to be worth pursuing. Lavochkin himself went into what appears to have been a creative decline after the war. Running second in state competitions for new aircraft against the designs of Artem Ivanovich Mikoyan, his design bureau shut up shop on his death in 1960.

A factory-fresh Russian Lavochkin La-7 in Moscow in 1945.

The other outstanding Soviet fighter of the Great Patriotic War was the Yak-3. This pretty little aircraft served a rather different role than that of the La-7. Where Lavochkin's fighter was used increasingly as an interceptor, the Yak-3 was used mostly as a tactical fighter, flying low over battlefields and engaging in dogfights below 13,000 feet. Like the La-7, the Yak-3 made its maiden flight in October 1943 and went into service in July 1944. It was an altogether smaller, lighter and more nimble machine than its predecessor, the Yak-1. Production accelerated rapidly, so that by mid-1946, 4,848 had been built, and yet relatively few Yak-3s saw action against the Luftwaffe.

By all accounts this was a delightful machine to fly; so much so that in 1991 the Museum of Flying in Santa Monica, California, approached Yakovlev in Orenburg, Russia, with the idea of producing a new series of Yak-3s for the civilian market. Built using original plans, tools, dies and fixtures, but fitted with Allison V-1710 engines, the new aircraft were snapped up by wealthy American enthusiasts.

The original aircraft had something of the look of the Spitfire about them. The Yakovlev team had some familiarity with Mitchell's marvel, but the design and development of liquid-cooled, V12-engined monoplane fighters had been following their own logic in the Soviet Union at a time when the British aircraft was all but unknown. Powered by a 1,290-hp Klimov VK-105PF-2 V12 (and, too late to see action, by a 1,650-hp VK-107A V12), the lightweight Yak climbed well and had a maximum speed of 407 mph (447 mph with the VK-107A). It was armed with one 20mm ShVAK cannon firing through the propeller hub, and two 12.7-mm UBS machine-guns.

On 14 July 1944, a flight of eighteen Yak-3s encountered thirty Luftwaffe fighters, destroying fifteen for the loss of one of their own. This was astonishing stuff, but far from a fluke. The Luftwaffe issued a warning to its pilots not to engage in low-level combat 'with Yakovlev fighters lacking an air-cooler under the nose'. This was a reference to the slower and less agile Yak-1. This is not to belittle the Yak-1, which was a fine aircraft; the Yak-3 was simply much quicker and more nimble.

The plywood Yak-3 was much liked by pilots and ground crew alike. It was robust, easy to maintain and a highly successful dogfighter, although unresolved wartime problems included glued-on plywood wing surfaces coming unstuck when the aircraft was pulled out of a high-speed dive. Its range, however, was limited. Yak-3s flew with the Czech and Polish Air Forces as well as the VVS after the war ended. They had also been the darlings of the Free

French pilots who fought with distinction with the Russians from 1943 onwards. These pilots included the official top-scoring Second World War French ace (twenty-three victories), Marcel Albert, a Parisian who now lives in Florida. Albert had flown Dewoitine D 520s in the Battle of France and Spitfires with 340 Squadron in England, before setting sail with some sixty fellow countrymen to the USSR, where they formed the Normandie-Niemen group. Most of his kills were made flying Yak-3s. Albert insists that the Yak-3 was a superior aircraft to the P-51D Mustang and, of course, to the Spitfire. He was, he has said, not impressed with the Spitfire at all. Of course not: it was perfidiously English; he was quintessentially French.

As for Alexander Sergeyevich Yakovlev, the much-decorated designer continued a very successful jet-age career, as well as serving as a deputy of the Supreme Soviet of the USSR from 1946 until his death in 1989. He retired from his own design bureau in 1984, sixty years after he had built his first aircraft.

At home, the Spitfire had no real rivals. However, because the Hawker Hurricane performed well and had entered production before the Spitfire, and because both the Air Ministry and the RAF were unsure as to whether or not Supermarine's fighter could be produced effectively and in sufficient volume, greater numbers of Sydney Camm's monoplane were in service at the start of the Second World War than Mitchell's. Hawker Hurricane enthusiasts are quick to rally to their cause. Hurricanes did indeed shoot down many more enemy aircraft than the Spitfire during the Battle of Britain, but then many more Hurricanes than Spitfires flew in the Battle of Britain. The victory to loss ratio of the two machines was close, although marginally in favour of the Spitfire. In any case, the aircraft, while they tackled anything that came their way, were broadly divided in their roles: the Spitfire's speed and handling made it an ideal fighter interceptor, while the robust and steady Hurricane tackled bombers. And it was no surprise, really, that the Spitfire won greater attention. The Hurricane had the appearance of a machine marking the end of a design tradition dating back to the First World War, while the Spitfire had the look of something entirely new. A Hurricane could never have flown as fast as a Spitfire. It was a fine machine, but as the years progressed it proved no match for Mitchell's masterpiece.

Camm himself, two years older than Mitchell, was a highly innovative and successful aero-engineer. His designs included the Second World War Typhoon and Tempest, the exquisite Hunter jet fighter of the 1950s and the P.1127 prototype of the Harrier jump-jet. The Hurricane could claim the distinction of being Britain's first monoplane fighter, but it was also just that little bit prior in every way to the Spitfire and so just that little bit less sophisticated. Its wings and fuselage were initially made out of timber ribs with linen fabric stretched over them, with aluminium-covered steel tubing being used for the cockpit frame-work and engine mounting. Joints were mechanically fastened rather than welded, as with the Spitfire. All this made the Hurricane much more of a known production quantity than the Spitfire, while RAF mechanics would also feel more at home with it. The Hurricane was a heavier aircraft than the Spitfire and so, equipped with the same 1,030-hp Rolls-Royce Merlin engine, it was, at 324 mph, the slower of the two. Although it was not to be developed to anything like the extent the Spitfire was during the Second World War, the Hurricane was a simple and sturdy machine that was put into mass production well in time to meet the German threat in 1939–40.

Design work on the Hurricane occupied Camm and his team at Kingston-upon-Thames, Surrey, for much of 1934. The prototype first flew from Brooklands on 6 November 1935 and the Hurricane Mk I entered RAF service in December 1937, with 111 Squadron. As a publicity stunt, and with a strong tail wind pushing him like the hand of God, Squadron Leader J. W. Gillan flew one of the squadron's Hurricanes from Edinburgh to Northolt aerodrome, Middlesex, at a remarkable average speed of 408 mph.

Improvements, among them metal-covered wings and armour plating, were made before the outbreak of war, by which time 497 Hurricanes had been built, equipping eighteen squadrons. As the war progressed and Spitfires replaced Camm's fighter at home, Hurricanes were sent to fight from Malta and further afield, in both the Middle East and Far East, where they met with great success. Fitted with two 40-mm cannon, Hurricane IIDs became highly effective tank-busters. Production continued up until February 1944, by which time 14,533 Hurricanes and Sea Hurricanes had been made, a sizeable number by Gloster Aircraft, others by the Canadian Car & Foundry Company (CCF), Montreal, and 300 by the Austin Motor Company. In September 1944, the prototype Hawker Sea Fury, the last of the great piston-engined fighters, made its maiden flight. Too late to see action in the Second World War, it was capable of 460 mph and went on to duel with Soviet MiG-15 jets in the Korean War.

Like the Mk I Spitfire, the Hurricane Mk I was fitted with eight wing-mounted .303 Browning machine-guns. It was much preferred as a gun platform as the aircraft was steadier and not so prone to the effects of recoil from the guns as the Spitfire. A major improvement in performance was made in September 1940 when the Hurricane Mk II went into service. This was powered by the

Merlin Mk XX with its two-stage supercharger boosting maximum power to 1,280 hp and the aircraft's top speed to 340 mph. The Mk IIA Series 2 of October 1940 could be armed with up to twelve Brownings or four Hispano 20-mm cannon. The Mk II was used successfully as a fighter-bomber and ground-attack aircraft as successive Spitfire marks chased the ever faster and more dangerous variants of the Luftwaffe's Bf 109 and Fw 190. The Mk IV could carry a pair of bombs and eight 60-lb RP-3 rockets. Power was up to 1,620 hp. Nevertheless the drag caused by bombs and rockets was considerable and the heavily laden late-mark Hurricanes were often slow and so easy prey to flak. A more powerful Mk V was designed to overcome this problem, but by this time the faster and altogether more powerful Hawker Typhoon had arrived to take over the most demanding ground-attack roles.

The Sea Hurricane Mk IA, or Hurricat, was launched from catapults on board merchant ships and used principally for the defence of convoys. Because the aircraft could not be recovered, they were often older aircraft converted for the purpose. Once launched, they blazed into action, and when the fuel ran out, their pilots bailed out and waited to be picked up by one of the ships they were protecting. A more sophisticated Mk IB Sea Hurricane was flown to and from merchant ships equipped with small flight decks able to carry a single fighter.

The top Hurricane ace was Frank Carey, the son of a builder from Brixton, south London, who shot down twenty-eight enemy aircraft. Other Hurricane aces, including Robert Stanford Tuck and Marmaduke Pattle, had higher scores, yet theirs, unlike Carey's, included victories made while flying other machines. The Hurricane was flown not only by the RAF, but also by the Forces

Aériennes Françaises Libres (the Free French Air Force) and the Irish Air Corps as well as by the air forces of Australia, Belgium, Canada, Egypt, Finland, India, New Zealand, Persia, Portugal, Romania, South Africa, the Soviet Union, Turkey and Yugoslavia. Sydney Camm died in 1966. His boss, Tommy Sopwith, designer of the famous First World War biplane fighter, the Sopwith Camel, lived on to 1989. I interviewed him that year. He was 101.

The Spitfire may have had the better of the Hurricane, but there was one Allied fighter that proved to be its equal, and even its superior, in certain ways. In 1939, the United States had no fighter aircraft that could match the Spitfire, yet it was soon to produce one of the finest piston-engined fighters of all time. The sleek North American P-51D Mustang was bigger, tougher, sturdier and, somehow, sexier than the Spitfire, and it was to influence the design of late-model versions of the British fighter including the Spiteful. The Mustang went on to play a major role as a ground-attack fighter in the Korean War, flew with the USAF until 1957, saw action as late as 1969, in the war between Honduras and El Salvador, and remained in service with South American air forces certainly into the 1980s and possibly into the following decade.

The Mustang remains a thrilling sight, and sound, and is a joy to fly, but perhaps the most intriguing thing about the P-51 is that it was always, in the happiest sense of the word, a mutt or mongrel. Either word will do as the Mustang was a fusion of American and British engineering inspiration and know-how, and it would never have existed if the RAF had not been looking to buy US fighters to fly alongside its Hurricanes and Spitfires. Through the Ministry of Air Production, the RAF ignited the development of the Mustang in 1939 when Sir Henry Self, who had worked with

Sir Wilfrid Freeman, the RAF officer who had directed the first order from Supermarine for 310 Spitfires three years earlier, was charged by the Ministry with the purchase of US fighter aircraft for the RAF. The design of US fighters lagged behind that of their European counterparts at the time and Self believed that only the Curtiss P-40 promised to be a worthwhile buy. While in the States, though, Self was approached by James H. 'Dutch' Kindleberger, president of North American Aviation, California, who promised he could deliver the goods. 'Dutch' must have impressed: the British placed an order for 320 North American fighters in March 1940 before Kindleberger's design team had even set to work on the future P-51.

That team was led by Edgar Schmued and Raymond Rice, who had the first P-51 up and flying, with an Allison 1710 engine, on 26 October 1940. This was startlingly quick work, and offered an early glimpse of the sheer industrial muscle that the US would flex as it pursued victory over the Axis powers. Kindleberger himself had learned much about production techniques from the Germans. In 1938, he visited the Heinkel and Messerschmitt factories, taking copious notes. He was soon to beat his German rivals at their own, highly efficient game. Nonetheless, the RAF found their P-51A Mustangs underpowered when they went into combat in May 1942. They flew well and were well made, but their Allison engines ran out of puff at much above 10,000 feet. These first Mustangs, then, could not be committed with anything like confidence against Bf 109s and Fw 190s. Instead, they were used mostly for ground-attack sorties.

The secret to revolutionizing the P-51's performance – and to turning it into the legendary fighter it became – was really no secret at all. Just three months after North American received its first order for 320 P-51As, the Rolls-Royce Merlin had gone into production under licence with Packard in Detroit. Meanwhile, Rolls-Royce's engineers at Hucknall had re-engined four RAF Mustangs with Merlin 61s and 65s and its pilots had undertaken exhaustive tests of this new combination of American airframe and British engine. The results indicated a dramatic all-round improvement in performance, especially at altitude. Now the Americans were impressed too and orders rolled in for the radically transformed fighter from the USAAF. From August 1943, this second generation of P-51B and C Mustangs – the former built at Inglewood, California, and the latter in a new plant at Dallas, Texas – roared into action with two-stage supercharged Packard-Merlin 68 engines mounted in their noses. And now at last, from December 1943, both the RAF and the fifteen fighter groups that were part of the Eighth and Ninth US Army Air Forces in England, and the Twelfth and Fifteenth in Italy, could provide their bombers with fighter escorts all the way to their targets over Germany and back again.

One major criticism of the P-51B and C from pilots was poor visibility, so in March 1944 the definitive P-51D Mustang emerged with a new teardrop canopy and cut-down rear fuselage. It was powered by a 1,695-hp Merlin and mounted six 0.5-inch Browning machine-guns in its wonderfully smooth laminar-flow wings. With a top speed of 437 mph, a ceiling of 41,900 feet and a range, with drop tanks, of 1,895 miles, the Mustang now posed a real challenge to even the best German fighters. It also kept Spitfire development up to the mark: the P-51D looked so very modern when compared to earlier Mustangs and was clearly a generation on in design terms from the Hurricane, the Curtiss P-40 and even the Spitfire. Towards the end of the war with Japan, the P-51H Mustang was on the verge of entering service. It sported a lightweight airframe and had a top speed of 487 mph, but just 555 were built by the time of the Japanese surrender and none flew in action. There was also to be a Twin Mustang, the F-82, which, like the Messerschmitt Bf 109Z, mated two fighter fuselages with a new centre wing. Originally intended as an escort fighter, the F-82 was later adapted to serve as a night- and all-weather fighter, and in this role it saw action in Korea.

The P-51D proved itself highly effective as a bomber escort, free-roaming interceptor and ground-attack aircraft. It was fast enough to intercept V1s, while Chuck Yeager, later the first pilot to break the sound barrier, was flying a P-51D when he became the first US pilot to shoot down an Me 262. Approximately half of all enemy aircraft destroyed in Europe by US fighters were the victims of P-51s; these included the earlier P-51B and C models which continued in action alongside the P-51D until the end of the war. By 8 May 1945, Mustang pilots had shot down approx-imately 4,950 enemy aircraft over Europe, the most claimed by any Allied fighter in air-to-air combat. The top Mustang ace was the USAAF's George Preddy, whose tally stood at 27.5 – twenty-four scored with the P-51 – when he was brought down and killed by friendly fire on 25 December 1944 during the Battle of the Bulge.

The RAF took delivery of about 2,600 Mustangs, which served in thirty-one squadrons in Britain and the Mediterranean. The last were withdrawn in November 1946. P-51D Mustangs, mean-while, were manufactured under licence in Australia by the Commonwealth Aircraft Company, Fisherman's Bend, Victoria, and the Australian Air Force had as many as 500 on its books at one time. A number of these were flown in the Korean War.

Other operators of the P-51, of which a total of 15,875 were made, included the air forces of Bolivia, Canada, China, Cuba (three flew with Fidel Castro's guerrilla forces in the Revolutionary War of 1956–9), Dominican Republic (until at least 1984), El Salvador, France, Guatemala, Haiti, Honduras, Indonesia, Israel, Italy, the Netherlands, Nicaragua, New Zealand, the Philippines, Somalia, South Africa, South Korea, Sweden, Switzerland, Taiwan and Uruguay. (The Soviet Union had tested a small number of early-model Mustangs, but these did not see frontline service.) Approximately 280 P-51s survive, of which more than half fly.

There were other impressive Second World War fighters, both Allied and Axis, that might be thought of as rivals to the Spitfire, among them the Hawker Tempest, Lockheed P-38 Lightning and Republic P-47 Thunderbolt. But the Tempest, although undoubtedly fast, powerful and an efficient despatcher of both V1s and Me 262s, was a relative latecomer, only entering RAF service in April 1944, and it was not built in great numbers. Meanwhile, the Lightning was a twin-engined machine and a long-range interceptor, very different in concept from the Spitfire, and the Herculean P-47 was really to find its true vocation as a fighter-bomber. As a fighter in the purest sense of the term, the Spitfire was, ultimately, in a class of its own. Designed in the mid-1930s as a short-range interceptor charged with the defence of Britain, it developed, and with remarkable speed, into a jack of all trades and a serious competitor to every new fighter produced throughout the Second World War.

The story might have been very different if Messerschmitt had been able to supply the Luftwaffe with Me 262 jet fighters two or even three years earlier. But it was not to be, and thank God for that, since skies full of German jet fighters would have wrought havoc. The agile Spitfire might have been able to get the better of an Me 262 in a dogfight, but its sheer speed would have made the jet a very demanding proposition had it been deployed in significant numbers. Even so, no Me 262 flew faster than a Spitfire in a dive, and no other fighter flew or fought so successfully before, through and well after the Second World War. I am prejudiced, of course, yet I remain convinced that the facts speak for themselves: the Spitfire was not only the finest fighter of its era but also one of the best aircraft that has ever flown.

CHAPTER VI

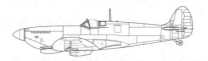

THE SPITFIRE SPIRIT

THE summer of 1940 transformed the Spitfire from a singularly good-looking and fine-handling fighter into a legend, the stuff of myth. The elliptical wings of the aircraft appeared, as many observers have noted, to spell 'victory' as surely and as confidently as Winston Churchill's famous two-fingered salute. Mitchell's fighters looked and sounded terrific as they swept over Kentish wealds and downs. Quite simply, the Spitfire stole hearts away. It was, and remains, one of those charismatic machines, like Nigel Gresley's 'The Flying Scotsman' or Malcolm Sayer's D-Type Jaguar, that look fast, lithe and purposeful at rest and refuse to disappoint when on the go. Like them, too, it is full of life and character – and seductive in its own mechanical way. Today, it seems almost a miracle that a country that finds it hard to make a railway locomotive, desires mostly to make money rather than anything worthwhile, and that has little respect for either engineers or factory workers, could produce an aircraft that was the envy of the world.

The sheer beauty and rightness of the Spitfire make us love it still. In the public imagination, and no matter how doughty the role played by the Hawker Hurricane, it was the Spitfire that 'won' the Battle of Britain. Mitchell's machine looked the part, just as Errol Flynn made a perfect Hollywood Robin Hood. Its name was just the ticket too. *Spitfire* had been the name of at least three Royal Navy warships, one of which, sold off in 1825, had fought alongside Nelson at the Battle of Trafalgar. Another HMS *Spitfire*, an Acasta-class destroyer, had taken part in the tumultuous Battle of Jutland in the First World War. The word evokes a feisty and venomous fighter. It was also a name that had been in the air, and on the big screen, at much the same time as Sir Robert McClean, chairman of Vickers, had suggested it for the new Supermarine fighter. Katharine Hepburn had played the lead in a Hollywood film entitled *Spitfire*, released in 1934. It is not a very good film, and the elegantly preppy Miss Hepburn was not exactly a hot-blooded spitfire in the accepted sense of the word. The better contender for this title, on celluloid anyway, was fiery Lupe Velez, a tiny, curvaceous Mexican actress. She starred in *The Mexican Spitfire* (1940) and five other films with 'spitfire' in the title. Or perhaps McClean was indeed thinking of his sparky young daughter at the time of the Hepburn film – after all, well-spoken Kate did seem a rather well-mannered and even very English 'spitfire'. But what matters is that the word was clearly in vogue, on the tip of the public's tongue.

Being so elegant, as well as fast, powerful and effective, the Spitfire was also a very British star. It was the fighter aircraft equivalent of the proverbial iron fist in velvet glove. It was also, to stretch the point a little, an aerial racehorse, a Pegasus-like machine that one could imagine, in a flight of fancy, careering through a scene of prize mounts painted by George Stubbs, the celebrated eighteenth-century English artist. In post-war years, the design ethos of the Spitfire could be found in such prize-winning English machines as the D-Type Jaguar, which first turned a very rapid wheel in 1954. Designed for William Lyons by the aerodynamicist Malcolm Sayer, the sensuous D-Type has often been referred to as a road- or track-going Spitfire. D-Types won the Le Mans Twenty-Four Hours motor race three times in the 1950s, trouncing their German and Italian rivals. I know these 170-mph cars well, and they really do live up to their reputation. If the D-Type had been called the Jaguar Spitfire, surely no one would have minded. The Spitfire spirit was, by then, part and parcel of the best and most sporting British engineering design.

As it was, another British car was to benefit from the name. The little Triumph Spitfire sports car, of which some 314,000 were made between 1962 and 1980, was an attempt to create a little of the essence of the Spitfire in the life of those on small budgets. Designed, and redesigned over the years, by the Italian stylist Giovanni Michelotti, the Spitfire was often advertised with the spirit of its famous namesake flying over its cramped cabin. Early adverts for the American export market boasted, 'You'd be proud, too…if your name was Spitfire,' and signed off with 'And nothing, but nothing looks like the Spitfire … except maybe that plane'. With a top speed of 92 mph and acceleration from rest to 50 mph in twelve seconds, the Triumph Spitfire was not exactly fast. Yet it was a nippy machine sold on the back of the enduring myth of Mitchell's masterpiece. It was, in effect, an updated version of the kind of lithe open-top English sports cars Spitfire pilots were always supposed to drive, even though in reality they drove, or rode, anything they could lay their hands on.

The actual experience of driving one of these little cars, if indeed they can be compared to aircraft, is more akin to that of piloting an open-cockpit First World War fighter – a Sopwith

Camel, say – than a sleek and superfast Second World War Spitfire. The point, though, is that when the Triumph was launched in 1962, there were plenty of young men, and women, who would have liked to have been, if only in their imaginations, at the controls of a Supermarine Spitfire, but were happy to accept the Triumph Spitfire as the closest they would ever get to the aerial legend.

Just how quickly the Spitfire became a popular legend can be measured by the speed with which it starred not just in wartime newsreels from the breathless studios of Pathé and Movietone but in a full-length feature film on general release. This was *The First of the Few* (1942). Leslie Howard, the ever so English actor best known for playing stiff-upper-lipped characters in such films as *Berkeley Square* (1933), *The Scarlet Pimpernel* (1934) and *Gone with the Wind* (1939), both directed and starred as R. J. Mitchell. His co-star, playing the thinly disguised role of Supermarine test pilot Jeffrey Quill, was the young and suave actor David Niven.

Howard had been born Leslie Howard Stainer to Jewish parents, his father Hungarian, his mother English. He had every good reason to wish to make a film about Mitchell, the Spitfire and those who were to fly it in action. Howard had been a soldier himself, serving in the First World War before being invalided out suffering from severe shell-shock. He was to die on his return from a secret mission to Lisbon in 1943 when the aircraft in which he was flying was shot down by the Luftwaffe over the Bay of Biscay. It is possible that the Germans thought Winston Churchill was on board.

The First of the Few is a very English film. It was, of course, propaganda, but directed with a light touch. Howard is depicted as the slightly misjudged genius battling illness – though not the cancer that killed the real 'R J' – as he struggles to design and build the fighter that will defeat the Nazis just as his floatplane racers had beaten the very best the Italians could offer during the years of the Schneider Trophy. Mitchell had in reality been working on other projects and, in particular, on the design of a fast, four-engined bomber, the Supermarine 316/7, in the last months of his life. He was also a much more irascible character, if no less stubborn, than the one portrayed by Howard. His domestic set-up, the design of his garden, indeed everything about the on-screen character, was carefully orchestrated to evoke the kind of decency that all English – and British – people were meant to be fighting for in the struggle against tyranny.

The script of the film took generous, if understandable, liberties. It had Mitchell travelling to Germany and meeting Willy Messerschmitt in a traditional inn, something he never did. Inevitably, it features the Germans as either scheming bullies or fleshy, oompah-band yokels, and the Italians as fat, preposterous and rather comic nincompoops. *The First of the Few* is nevertheless a touching and appropriately stirring film. From the beginning, it depicts a country infused with a spirit of inspired amateurishness, intelligence and resolve, that will surely defeat braggarts, Fascists and Nazis. And if the bantering Spitfire pilots shown in the opening sequence seem altogether too amateur as actors, it is because they were the real thing: young RAF pilots making an awkward bow while celebrating their finest hour.

As for David Niven, he was not at all like Jeffrey Quill, a serious, terrier-like fellow and one of the greatest and bravest of all test pilots. None of this would have mattered in 1942, and it hardly matters decades later. When Niven's character leans out of the cockpit of his Spitfire at the end of the film and cries, 'They can't take the Spitfires, Mitch. They can't take them!' it seems, if a little

A poster for Leslie Howard's film *The First of the Few*, released in the US as *Spitfire*.

cheesy, perfectly all right. Messerschmitt's Bf 109s flown well could take them, of course, but this was good-hearted propaganda. It struck the right chord and is still moving, even if in a slightly awkward way, today.

The First of the Few was released in the United States as *Spitfire*. The name was well on its way to becoming a universal symbol, not just of British but of global defiance against despotism. The Sicilian-born Frank Capra (1897–1991), meanwhile, directed an Academy Award-winning series of wartime Hollywood documentaries, *Why We Fight*. This included *The Battle of Britain*

(1943), in which the Spitfire played another starring role. Most Americans were broadly supportive of their country's war with Japan, following the attack on Pearl Harbor in December 1941, but many remained sceptical about the reasons for the expenditure of so many resources, and so many lives, as the United States fought in what seemed to be no more than a squabble for power in an old and distant Europe. The Spitfire was as potent a symbol as any with which to win American hearts and minds.

Perhaps the most beautiful evocation of the form, spirit and purpose of the Spitfire on film at the time was made in *A Canterbury Tale* (1944), directed by Michael Powell and Emeric Pressburger. This was Chaucer's medley of short stories brought up to date for, and made pointedly relevant to, a wartime audience. It opens with a sequence depicting the progress of a band of medieval pilgrims through the English countryside. A hooded falcon sits on the wrist of one of the pilgrims until it is unleashed in pursuit of a pigeon. When no more than a pin prick in the sky, the bird of prey is seen turning, and then roars back towards the camera in the guise of a Spitfire, its Merlin engine in full song.

By then, the Spitfire had become far more than a machine. It was a symbol of Britain's lone defiance against Hitler in 1940–41, and the nation's gift to allies fighting totalitarianism in other parts of the world. It was William Blake's 'bow of burning gold' drawn over 'England's green and pleasant land'. It was a crusader fighting to establish a New Jerusalem upon hills clouded by war. Significantly, this is what many British people, including the majority of soldiers, really were fighting for in their various ways by the end of the Second World War. When they voted out Churchill in favour of Clement Attlee and his socialist Labour government in the general election of 1945, it was not so much a snub to the great wartime leader as a rejection of the world of economic depression and class distinction that the Tories had seemed to epitomize in the years leading up to the war. A clear majority of the electorate wanted the land for the commonplace, everyday heroes for whom the Spitfire had fought, both symbolically and in fierce action.

By the early 1950s, though, Britons were more concerned with getting on with the rest of their lives: they had very much come down to earth after all the terrors and thrills of the war – just as the Spitfire itself had been largely withdrawn from frontline service. You were far more likely to find one mounted on a pedestal outside an RAF base than chasing an enemy through footless halls of air. *Angels One Five* (1952), directed by George More O'Ferrall, reflects the different times. It tells the story of the Battle of Britain as experienced, and reported, by those on the ground at an RAF airfield. There is, in fact, little aerial action. Fittingly perhaps for a film made when post-war rationing was still in force, *Angels* is gritty, dogged, black-and-white, decidedly unromantic and pretty realistic; the role of the Group Controller was played by ex-Squadron Leader Ronald Adam, former Group Controller at Hornchurch.

It was equally difficult to find Spitfires – or Hurricanes, come to that – for *Reach for the Sky* (1956), a black-and-white feature directed by Lewis Gilbert and celebrating the life of Douglas Bader, the tin-legged champion of Big Wing formations of fighters during and after the Battle of Britain. A number of post-war Spitfires were drafted in for the flying sequences, and good use was made of film shot by Spitfires' gun cameras in the summer of 1940. Sadly, I find this film hard to watch. Perhaps Kenneth More's rather romanticized Bader, a blend of bullying bluster and jolly-good-show humour, was all too reminiscent of the hectoring schoolmasters who, no doubt unintentionally, encouraged me to stare out of high classroom windows at the sky during lessons or to doodle Spitfires gunning down Messerschmitts and Stukas in my exercise books. I am sure that *Reach for the Sky* is somehow uplifting and an inspiration to the physically disabled; but it also seems insufferably smug.

By the 1960s, Britain was set on a course of huge social change. As Harold Macmillan had proclaimed, many of us really had never had it so good, and a generation was coming of age that had no memory of the particular horrors and grimness of a world war. We had become neophiliacs, more interested in the Mini and the mini, in sex and the end of censorship, in the Beatles and the Rolling Stones, than in reliving the war – until, that is, we beat West Germany in the final of the 1966 World Cup.

It was not until the very end of the decade that the Spitfire once again featured prominently on the big screen. *Battle of Britain* (1969), directed by Guy Hamilton, was intended to be the definitive British film of the great event. It falls far short of this lofty aim, however, and is very patchy indeed, never seeming to know quite whether it is meant to be set in 1940 or the late 1960s. Accents and haircuts are as uncertain as the aircraft themselves, with anachronistic, late-mark Spitfires battling Spanish Air Force Hispano HA-1112 Buchons masquerading as Bf 109s. This could be forgiven as by this time there were very few Spitfires in flying order and no original Bf 109s. Remarkably, though, the production team, led by Harry Saltzman and S. Benjamin Fisz, garnered no fewer than twenty-seven Spitfires, of which a dozen could fly. They also rustled up six Hurricanes, three of them airworthy, and from Spain seventeen Buchons and two Ju 52 transport planes. They also earmarked no fewer than thirty-two Spanish-built Heinkel He 111H twin-engined bombers, although just two of these were actually used for filming. Half-scale, remote-controlled Junkers Ju 87 Stuka dive-bombers and He 111s were built, mostly so that they could be shot down. Brand-new Aston-Martins, Jaguars and a Lamborghini Miura might have been wilfully destroyed in *The Italian Job* (1969), a British comedy-thriller starring Michael Caine and, of course, the Mini, but no one was going to destroy authentic Second World War aircraft. Many other Spitfires and Hurricanes shown in the film were mock-ups, some equipped with engines from lawn-mowers, so that they could taxi around an airfield which was a cut-and-paste mix of Duxford, Debden, Hawkinge and North Weald.

Above all, *Battle of Britain* lacked authenticity. Everyone seemed too well-groomed, too long-haired and too well-fed. Cars and lorries, aircraft even, were too clean. It was impossible to believe in Caine, however good he had been in other films of the time, as an RAF officer. Only Laurence Olivier rose to the occasion, imbuing the role of Air Chief Marshal 'Stuffy' Dowding with just the right mix of reserve and quietly concealed passion. It also helped that Olivier could stand where Dowding used to, looking up at the sky from the balcony outside his office at Bentley Priory.

The aerial sequences, filmed from a North American B-25 Mitchell wartime bomber painted a lurid green and pink, were excellent, however, and they did much to encourage the burgeoning Spitfire revival, which was to see a whole small industry grow up around the restoration of Mitchell's fighter over the following two decades. If *Battle of Britain* was flawed, it none-theless spurred Spitfires back into flight to take part in further films and television series as well as air shows around the world.

Over three decades later, aerial footage from Hamilton's film was reused in *Dark Blue World* (2001), a tale of two Czech pilots who escape Nazi-occupied Europe to fly with the RAF during the Battle of Britain. Both are imprisoned by the new communist regime when they return home after the war. The film was something of a curate's egg, and the best parts were undoubtedly the aerial scenes, for which director Jan Sverák had filmed some impressive new sequences. Up close, the Spitfires looked and sounded glorious: it was a wonder to watch spent Browning .303 cartridges falling, with a clatter, from the undersides of their wings. Such detail was terrific, even if the film as a whole was somehow unconvincing. Perhaps it was the locations. Rural Czechoslovakia was clearly very beautiful, but it could not and would not stand in for wartime Kent.

Sverák had intended to make a film about the lives of the pilots involved, their loves, their politics, their twinned fates, with less emphasis on the aircraft. Filming Spitfires at the end of the twentieth century was, in any case, an expensive pursuit. But Sverák too fell in love with the Spitfire when his cameras rolled and he saw, heard and framed them in full cry for the first time. 'One Spitfire,' he said at the time of the film's release, 'costs about $10,000 per hour, so every minute of flying time means a lot of money out of the budget. Each time a plane was to land, an inner struggle would take hold of me – the little boy in me wanted to watch the amazing machine fly a little bit longer and the adult producer worried about the extra $650 for another round. In the end I always said to myself, let him do another turn. The Spitfire produces a very special sound and when it flies over your head, when you hear the engine for the first time, you appreciate its awesome power. It feels like attending a Mass.'

Sverák's editors cut computer-generated sequences into the flying scenes. Despite its high performance and superb handling characteristics, the Spitfire itself is still very much an analogue-era aircraft. When, a few years ago, I was forcibly made to join some young, digital-era boys in a computer game simulating a dogfight between Spitfires and Bf 109s, I performed very badly indeed: digitized aircraft seem just too remote from the real thing. I crashed a lot before I became bored and went off to walk the dogs under a magnificent winter sky more alive with the promise, and spirit, of a Supermarine Spitfire than any eye-straining computer screen could ever be.

In fact, the most successful attempt to give the Spitfire and the spirit that drove it some relevance to post-war children was made long before the advent of computer games or iPods. It took the form of the comic strip 'Dan Dare: Pilot of the Future' in *The Eagle*, a comic launched long before I was born, yet set well into the future.

First published in 1950, *The Eagle* was the brainchild of Marcus Morris, a Church of England priest and bon viveur turned publisher. He wanted to produce a comic that would instil Christian values in young boys, and the principal feature of his beautifully produced weekly was Colonel Dare, Space Fleet's top pilot. By his example, Dan Dare would help to promote the virtues of a muscular, and very decent, Christianity.

Whether this particular aspect of Morris's intentions was successful or not is anyone's guess. What we do know is that *The Eagle* was a publishing phenomenon, selling almost a million copies in its first week. What so many of us liked about Dan Dare is that, although his stories were meant to be set in the late 1990s, our clean-cut, lantern-jawed hero with the permanently quizzical

An advertisement announcing the return of Frank Hampson's 'Dan Dare' cartoon in *The Eagle*.

eyebrows was clearly a Battle of Britain Spitfire pilot. He spoke a slightly futuristic RAF banter – 'Suffering satellites!' – wore a classic Spitfire pilot's Irwin jacket, smoked a pipe and flew spaceships like the *Anastasia* that were space-age Spitfires. His commander, Sir Hubert Guest, modelled physically on the comic strip artist Frank Hampson's father, was a reincarnation of the RAF's Battle of Britain commander in chief, Hugh Dowding.

Dan Dare's greatest enemy was the Mekon, totalitarian leader of Venus and of the green, lizard-faced Treens, who obeyed orders at all times. The Mekon may have had a huge, bulbous head and a tiny body, and floated about on what looked like a streamlined tea-tray, but even the most dim-witted schoolboy would have realized that the Mekon was a stand-in for Hitler and that his Treens were Nazi storm-troopers from outer space. When asked what influence Dan Dare had had on him, Professor Stephen Hawking replied, 'Why am I in cosmology?' Dear, indestructible Colonel Dare was the embodiment of the ideal Spitfire pilot as seen through the eyes of a committed Christian editor, a brilliant cartoonist and the 1950s.

The Eagle not only offered this spiffing portrait of the Spitfire pilot but also did Mitchell's memory proud with its superb cutaway colour illustrations of Spitfires and many other British aircraft of the period, together with ships, cars, buses, locomotives and power stations. Morris's creation was very much part of the last flourish of a still credible notion that British engineering-led design was the best. Or at least as good as anything Johnny Foreigner could manage. Buoyed up by its success in the Second World War, Britain did have much to be proud of. In the eyes of *The Eagle*, our record-breaking jets, V-bombers, vertical take-off fighters, hover-craft and inter-continental ballistic missiles were all the natural successors to the Spitfire. Britain would surely be able to face an enemy single-handedly again, just as it had done in the summer of 1940.

The hopes, fears and events of that legendary Spitfire summer were to be more realistically recreated in the television series *Piece of Cake*, first screened in 1988 and based on a fine novel by Derek Robinson published five years earlier. Although Robinson's fictional Hornet Squadron flew Hurricanes, their replacement with Spitfires on TV made sense. There were very few airworthy Hurricanes to film, and the Spitfire was always going to be the bigger draw in terms of ratings. The series was made at a time when the conservation movement, whether in historic aircraft, classic cars or old buildings, was in full swing after the pop and pace of the 1960s and 1970s. In Britain, many of those who had grown up reading *The Eagle* now had plenty of money to spend on restoration projects: owning and flying a Spitfire had become a reality for an increasing number of wealthy enthusiasts. By 1988, the Spitfire was very much back in the public eye, or at least it was for those who enjoyed trekking to air shows or furtively reading copies of *Fly Past*, a magazine launched in 1981 and dedicated to the rescue of old 'warbirds', behind their broadsheet newspapers on the daily commute.

During the 1960s, the few Spitfires that flew were largely second-hand machines bought straight from service or restored RAF gate-guardians. There was a potential market for a healthy number of restored Spitfires even then, but insufficient funds or skills were available to take the aircraft safely back into the sky. This situation changed in 1980s Britain, when considerable fortunes were made in the City and in the property and insurance markets, encouraging a number of would-be Spitfire pilots to make their dream come true. Some were already keen classic car racing drivers, but the desire for ever greater thrills invariably proved irresistible. And what could make more sense than swapping the driver's seat of an old Bentley or Ferrari for the cockpit of a Spitfire? The Honourable Patrick Lindsay, a Christie's auctioneer and amateur racing driver, flew a fully restored Westland-built 1941 Mk Ia until his death in 1986. The aircraft's next owner, in 1989, was Victor Gauntlett, the exuberant chairman of Aston Martin, makers of some of the finest and fastest of all British cars. Gauntlett died in 2003. Charles Church, the well-known traditional English house-builder, went so far as to commission a brand-new Mk VC Spitfire, although sadly in 1989 he died flying this fine machine after it suffered an engine failure.

Meanwhile Jeffrey Quill, the former Supermarine test pilot, was pursuing a project to build an exact replica of K5054, the prototype Spitfire, to be put on permanent public display as a memorial to R. J. Mitchell. It was certainly as good a time as any to get the project off the ground. Quill's drive had already led to the formation of the Spitfire Society in 1983. A team of original Supermarine designers worked with Aerofab Restorations of Andover for ten years to create the facsimile. It was unveiled to the public in April 1993 by Quill at the RAF Museum, Hendon, and is currently on loan to the Tangmere Military Aviation Museum. All the photographs of K5054 are in black and white, and most of those that were not taken by Charles Brown are rather dull. But when you see the machine in its beautiful pale-blue colour scheme, it makes the heart leap and reminds visitors to Tangmere of just how extraordinarily futuristic Mitchell's fighter must have seemed in 1936.

Piece of Cake not only offered a brilliant, often caustic, depiction of what it was like to live, and sometimes die, as a fighter pilot, but it also brought the Spitfire very much back to life. The series included a number of memorable flying sequences made possible by amateur Spitfire pilots soaring over Hatfield House at lawn-mowing level, flying under a bridge in the Severn Valley and swooping up and over the white cliffs of Dover faster than any bluebird. In 1986, Herbie Knott of the then recently launched *Independent* newspaper was the stills photographer for the series, and two of his fine photographs are included in this book. I was also working for the *Independent* and was able to write about Spitfires on a number of occasions. Photo editors at this picture-led daily loved the shape of these machines just as much as I did, and it was easy to persuade them that there was just one more event worthy of national attention that merited another portrait of a Spitfire.

The legend and spirit of the Spitfire have, of course, been safeguarded in other ways over the decades, notably by the hugely popular injection-moulded plastic kits made by Airfix. This famous British company was founded in 1939 by Nicholas Kove, a Hungarian-born Jew. Kove turned to the manufacture of plastic models when F. W. Woolworth approached Airfix in 1953 with a proposal to supply its high-street shops with a model of Sir Francis Drake's sixteenth-century flagship, the *Golden Hind*. The tricky bit was that the model could not cost more than 2s (10 pence). Kove's joint managing director was Ralph Ehrmann, who, despite his very German-sounding name, had flown with RAF Bomber Command during the war, and his chief buyer John Gray was another former RAF hand and an expert in aircraft recognition.

Soon after, Airfix launched the first of its celebrated and very numerous 1/72-scale plastic model aircraft kits. This was the Spitfire. Its blue plastic parts were wrapped in a plastic bag stapled to a thick paper sheet which illustrated the aircraft and unfolded to reveal the instructions to enable schoolboys, and a few schoolgirls, to make a Spitfire of their very own. The kit, more or less a Battle of Britain Mk I, was not entirely accurate. But it was a reasonable representation of Mitchell's fighter and at just two shillings a pop it ensured that middle-class children at least could afford it with their weekly pocket money.

The result? The Spitfire became as ubiquitous as it had been a decade earlier. Now trailing threads of Britfix glue and camouflaged with Humbrol enamels, it was flown through living rooms, kitchens and bathrooms by very young and amateur pilots instead of 1940s Brylcreem Boys. It strafed cats and dogs, rabbits and guinea-pigs, and ratter-tatted through school playgrounds and public parks. Model Spitfires also started new wars, albeit this time on the domestic front. One of my sisters smashed a squadron of my lovingly assembled, painted and detailed Spitfires with a tennis racket under the mistaken impression that I had punctured her football. Such damaged aircraft, stuffed with cotton wool soaked in methylated spirits, met fiery ceremonial ends, catapulted from top-floor bedroom windows.

Airfix has produced some splendid Spitfires in its time. Its 1/24 Mk Ia effectively pioneered that imposing scale, and its more recent 1/48 Spitfire F 22/24 and Seafire Mk 46/47 are peerless. The company still survives – unlike its great British rivals, Frog and Matchbox – and is celebrating the Spitfire's seventieth in style. But it is not the polystyrene power it once was, and its latest offering, a Mk IX in 1/48 scale, even seems a tad crude when set

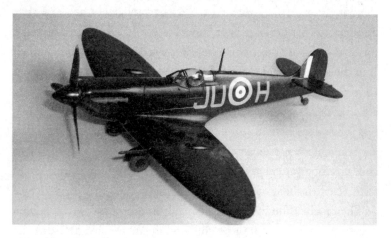

An Airfix 1/48 Spitfire Mk VB in the markings of 111 Squadron.

alongside the competition. Indeed, it is an abiding irony that the intricate – and ruinously expensive – moulds for many of the best Spitfire kits have been created and machined in the Far East, principally by the Japanese, our former allies in the First World War and enemies in the Second. However, the legend clearly lives on: an original 1950s Airfix Spitfire kit, still in its transparent plastic bag, is now worth at least £100.

Perhaps the Germans are right and the British have been obsessed for far too long with the Second World War. Certainly a steady stream of films, comics, television series, books and plastic kits has kept the war evergreen – and earth brown and duck-egg blue – in both our eyes and hands. There again, our stand against Hitler was a high point in our country's history, and what might have happened if we had not had Spitfires to guard us in the summer of 1940 really does not bear thinking about. And the memoirs keep coming. Geoffrey Wellum's surprise bestseller, *First Light* (2003), was the story – his own – of a teenage fighter pilot getting through the summer of 1940 in the hot seat of a Spitfire, and somehow surviving. It is beautifully told and, given Britain's far less innocent involvement in the invasion and occupation of Iraq, perhaps Wellum stirred up memories of what it was like to have fought as a wide-eyed young man in what has long, and quite rightly, been seen as a just war.

It is also the case, as Wellum reiterated, that for his generation the war was such an overwhelming experience that, however hard they tried to convince themselves otherwise, much of the rest of their lives was something of an anticlimax. The comedian Spike Milligan, who fought with the Eighth Army in North Africa, caught this feeling cleverly and cruelly in one of his typically unformed television sketches. He showed a crowd of cockney old age pensioners, bored with life and wishing for the good old days. Their dream comes true. In a flash, it's 1940 – the Blitz rages, bombs fall from the sky and several of the pensioners are blown to pieces.

Contemporary adverts for Spitfire Ale, brewed by Shepherd Neame at Faversham in Kent, have definitely not been tailored to German sensibilities. One, envisaging someone asking how to get to the nearest pub selling Spitfire ale, bellows, 'First left, then Third Reich'. Another is emblazoned with the blunt statement, 'Not for Messrs Schmidt'. The posters are signed off, 'The Bottle of Britain'.

As for the real machines, there are currently some fifty Spitfires flying today, a number that waxes and wanes as one aircraft is restored to airworthy condition and another crashes or retires for further restoration. There are peacetime Spitfire pilots who, like the late father and son team, Ray and Mark Hanna, both former RAF jet fighter jocks, became as well-known as their wartime predecessors. A growing number of companies, based in England, France, Australia, Canada and the United States, manufacture replica Spitfires. Some are tiny things with no more than 65 hp to play with; some boast Chevrolet V8 engines, others Japanese V6s. There are even full-scale machines available powered by 1,200-hp Allison V12s offering considerable performance. I cannot pretend to be a fan of such aircraft, even though the very first was designed and built by John Isaacs, a former Supermarine draughtsman. Yet there is clearly a market, worldwide, for would-be Spitfires that offer amateur pilots some ersatz sense of what it might have been like to fly the real thing in action. But if you cannot have a Supermarine Spitfire, why not settle for a De Havilland Tiger Moth or else one of a number of practical historic aircraft that fly

A Charles Brown portrait of a PR Mk XI Spitfire being tested by Jeffrey Quill in mid-1943.

beautifully yet have no pretensions to being anything like a Merlin- or Griffon-powered Spitfire?

Rebuilding original Spitfires is a small yet thriving industry. At the Imperial War Museum, Duxford, Historic Flying Ltd has undertaken slow but sure nut-and-rivet restorations since 1989. But only multi-millionaires need apply. A restoration costs up to £1.5 million – about three times the cost, in real terms, of building a Spitfire during the Second World War. There are those willing to spend this kind of money on what is, by the nature of the aircraft, a selfish pleasure. This, though, is understandable. The Spitfire itself, of whatever mark, remains a joy to fly, and while the Merlin-engined aircraft thrum smoothly through the air, their Griffon-powered siblings are like growling, bucking broncos.

The Spitfire continues to haunt our imagination. It has flown with us through seventy years of war and peace, and is inextricably bound up with so many of our family histories. Its mechanical brilliance and bounding curves are still a source of wonder, just as its achievements still make us feel both proud and profoundly grateful. Above all, it remains a symbol of freedom – of a belief in democracy, decency and the rule of law – and it encourages us to fight, fight and fight again against any government, even our own, which tries to bully us, lie to us or otherwise infringe our hard-won liberties. There is, one hopes, a Spitfire in every one of us.

EPILOGUE

'WHEN did you last fly a Spitfire?' I ask Diana Barnato-Walker as we settle down for toast and honey and Earl Grey tea in the drawing room of her late Victorian Surrey rectory. The spring gardens resound with birdsong. Beyond a field studded with her pedigree sheep, jet airliners criss-cross a bright cirrus sky on their approach to Gatwick airport a little way off beyond the tree line.

'Oh, last month,' says the Commodore of the Air Transport Auxiliary Association. 'A two-seater, with me in the back. I got my turn to fly. Would be impolite not to, don't you think?'

I do. At eighty-eight, Diana is evidently the same slim young beauty who was captured for posterity in the delightful photograph of her climbing into the cockpit of a Mk IX Spitfire in the spring of 1945. 'It was taken at RAF Hamble. I do wish I knew who the photographer was. The picture is out of copyright now, but he would have made a tidy bit from the number of times it has been reproduced.'

Outside of the Soviet Union, women did not fly in combat in the Second World War. 'I think we would have been perfectly decent fighter pilots,' Diana says, 'but it wasn't an issue we girls discussed. It was simply assumed that war was men's business. But we had a duty to back them up. Of course, this was no ordinary war. We had to do something to stop Hitler, for freedom, and for the Jews. We could hardly sit about looking pretty and doing nothing, could we?'

Slipped between the pages of Diana's crammed logbooks are photographs of her and her fellow women pilots posing on, alongside and in front of Spitfires. 'It was, beyond doubt, a wonderful aircraft,' she says. She should know. Diana flew 260 Spitfires from 1942 to 1945, among a fleet of other makes and types of aircraft – Gladiators, Beaufighters, Hurricanes, Mosquitoes, a Swordfish, Mustangs, Mitchells, Typhoons – delivering them from factories to squadrons.

'One is allowed, I think, to be proud of certain things in one's life,' she says. 'Do you know, I never crashed, never so much as scratched one of those Spitfires. Fresh from the factory and a brief flight by one of the test pilots, and up we'd go in all weathers. Unless Alex [Henshaw] had made the test flight, you'd find the settings all over the place. But you just had to get on with it. There was no time for fuss. The aircraft were needed urgently, and our young men were being killed.

'I liked the earlier marks the best. The first I flew were Mk IIs; they were light and nimble. Very responsive. I think that having ridden from a very young age helped a great deal. Climbing into the saddle of another new Spitfire was rather like getting into the saddle of an unfamiliar horse; but, if you were confident, you could get along with any of them pretty well. But all the Spitfires were fun to fly. How privileged I was to have flown so many.'

Diana was also the only woman ATA pilot to have flown across the Channel into occupied Europe. This was in September 1944 at the controls of a Mk IX. 'The enemy was fifteen miles the other side of our lines, so I didn't feel there was much to worry about. I'd faced more danger in England when, occasionally, one was attacked by a German fighter. In such circumstances, we were instructed to turn, full-throttle, inland. The German aircraft had such a short range that it was always madness for them to chase us; they needed the fuel to get back home.'

Other predators included the many RAF officers who were thrilled to see a well-groomed young lady stepping out of a new Spitfire. 'I always wore lipstick and brushed my hair before climbing out. Oh, the boys loved us. They were very supportive, but rather flirtatious. One CO made sure I stayed overnight by having the plugs removed from the aircraft I was to fly back in. I was too green then to have had a look under the bonnet and to see for myself what was wrong. In any case, I was still very much a girl of my times, and anything mechanical had always been sorted out for me. When my father presented me with a brand-new Bentley for my twenty-first birthday – it was parked outside the Ritz ready for when I woke up and looked out of the window – we took her for a spin up to Montmartre. I burned out the clutch. Father wasn't at all upset. He simply telephoned his friend, Ettore, who had the car returned to the Ritz as good as new in the evening. That was Ettore Bugatti, a charming man. I think I was rather spoilt.'

What changed Diana's life and saved her – the daughter of Woolf 'Babe' Barnato, one of the richest and most exciting men in England – from life in a gilded cage was the Spitfire. 'Here was something I could do usefully and pretty well: deliver the latest fighters. The war knocked the stuffing out of me. Before it, I had

A restored Spitfire Mk IX makes a low pass at Charlton Park, Gloucestershire, in 1987.

only moved in rather grand circles. Now, I got to muck in with everyone. I loved my new life as much as I loved Spitfires. And you have to remember that we were all terribly young and thrilled to be alive from day to day. Always felt the cold, though. So I swapped a little gold watch I had for that fleece-lined leather jacket you see in the photograph of me everyone seems to like so much. No, it wasn't a standard-issue RAF flight-crew jacket. I think it came from Afghanistan. Would you care to see it?'

From inside a cupboard under the stairs Diana extracts the very same, exceedingly well-worn jacket. It is more than sixty years old. 'I use it when I'm looking after the sheep, or tending the horses,' she says. 'It's been rather good value, don't you think?'

We go back to the drawing room for sherry. The walls are lined with paintings of hunting horses and with books on aircraft, racing cars, birds, art and architecture. Among the books is a copy of Le

Corbusier's extraordinary *Aircraft* (1934), in which the famous Swiss-French architect foresaw, if unintentionally, the ways in which the aircraft was about to destroy the venerable European cities it emerged from and flew over, laden with bombs and prickling with guns.

'Do you shoot?' asks Diana, fixing the rabbits prancing across her lawns with a hawk-like eye. 'Don't you like rabbit pie?' I look at this extraordinary woman. A good shot. A hunter. An acclaimed flyer. A refined and modest beauty. It might be an odd thought, yet to me Diana Barnato-Walker personifies the Supermarine Spitfire.

'It's funny how you can always recognize a pilot,' she says. 'Their eyes are always looking up and into the horizon. Now what sort of aircraft is that?' she asks of a Boeing 767 on its final descent into Gatwick. 'And do look at those robins landing in the ornamental cherry...' I half expect a Spitfire to come flying in salute over sheep and trees, robins and rectory. Symbol of freedom. Guardian of so many millions of lives worth living to the full. A deadly beauty. R. J. Mitchell's sky goddess.

TECHNICAL
SPECIFICATIONS

M ORE Spitfires were built than any other British fighter: the first in 1936, the last in 1947. During that time, there were at least forty-six different Spitfire marks or designations. This was an aircraft that continued to develop month by month as it faced new challenges and responded to the latest developments in aero-engines, armaments and airframe technology. Of the many Spitfire variations, aside from the prototype K5054, there were five key models – the Mk I, V, IX and XIV and the F 24 – and these are detailed below. Seafire variants follow. Dates refer to the first and the final placing of orders for production of a particular mark.

SPITFIRE

PROTOTYPE, K5054

July 1934

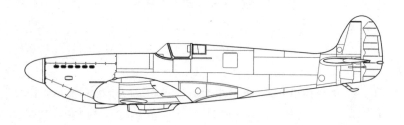

Total built: 1

Wingspan: **37 feet 8 inches**
Length: **29 feet 11 inches**
Empty weight: **3,979 lbs**
Loaded weight: **5,250 lbs**

Engine: **Rolls-Royce Merlin C liquid-cooled 27-litre V12**
Maximum power: **990 hp**
Maximum speed: **349 mph at 16,800 feet**

Service ceiling: **34,500 feet**
Climb to 20,000 feet: **8 minutes 12 seconds**
Rate of climb at 20,000 feet: **1,770 feet per minute**

Armament: **eight .303 Browning Mk II machine-guns**

MK I

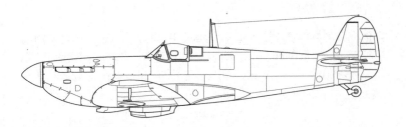

Total built: **1,577**

Wingspan: **36 feet 10 inches**
Length: **29 feet 11 inches**
Empty weight: **4,341 lbs**
Loaded weight: **5,720 lbs**

Engine: **Rolls-Royce Merlin II or III**
Maximum power: **1,030 hp**
Maximum speed: **362 mph at 18,500 ft**

Service ceiling: **34,500 feet**
Climb to 10,000 feet: **4 minutes 18 seconds**
Rate of climb at 20,000 ft: **2,195 feet per minute**

Typical armament:
Mk IA: **eight .303 Browning Mk II machine-guns**
Mk IB: **two 20-mm Hispano cannon and four .303 Browning machine-guns**

MK II   *April 1939*

Total built: **920**

The Mk II was built at the Castle Bromwich Aircraft Factory, Birmingham. It went into service during the Battle of Britain in August 1940. Very similar to the Mk 1, but with a number of minor improvements.

MK III   *Orders cancelled before production*

Total built: **2**

An attempt at a complete reworking of the Spitfire before its replacement with a new fighter. The 400-mph clipped-wing prototype, N3297, made its maiden flight on 15 March 1940. It was not altogether popular with test pilots, and was ousted by the highly successful Mk V.

MK IV   *Prototype*

Total built: **2**

This was the first Griffon-engined Spitfire; the aim was a 470-mph fighter armed with six 20-mm cannon. Jeffrey Quill made the first flight on 27 November 1941. It was later converted to a Mk XII. The second prototype became the basis of the F 21.

PR IV   *August 1940*

Total built: **229**

This was the first of the mass-produced, Merlin-powered photo-reconnaissance Spitfires. They carried extra fuel – between 228 and 247 gallons – and were equipped with either one or two heated cameras. They were unarmed.

MK V

August 1939–October 1941

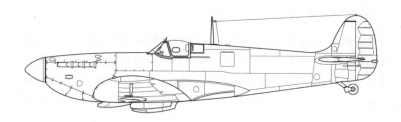

Total built: **6,787**

Wingspan: **36 feet 10 inches**
Length: **29 feet 11 inches**
Empty weight (Mk VB): **5,065 lbs**
Loaded weight (Mk VB): **6,525 lbs**

Engine: **Rolls-Royce Merlin 45, 45M, 46, 50, 50M or 56**
Maximum power: **1,440–1,470 hp**
Maximum speed (Mk VB): **371 mph at 20,000 ft**

Service ceiling: **37,500 feet**
Climb to 10,000 feet: **4 minutes 18 seconds**
Rate of climb at 20,000 feet: **2,440 feet per minute**

Typical armament (Mk VB): **four .303 Browning Mk II machine-guns and two 20-mm Hispano cannon**

MK VI   *August 1939*

Total built: **97**

A high-altitude interceptor with a pressurized cabin, elongated wings and ceiling of 39,000 feet, designed to meet the threat of a new generation of high-altitude German bombers over Britain that never materialized. Many, with wings clipped, were used as trainers.

MK VII   *October 1940*

Total built: **140**

A refined version of the Mk VI with a ceiling of 43,000 feet. The 1,710-hp Merlin 64 gave some Mk VIIs a maximum speed of 408 mph.

MK VIII   *January 1942*

Total built: **1,654**

A development of the Mk VII designed as an all-purpose interceptor. Built exclusively by Supermarine's own factories, the impressive Mk VIII had a performance similar to the Mk IX and saw service mainly in the Mediterranean and Far East and was flown in action by a number of Allied air forces. Six Mk VIIIGs were used for further tests with the Griffon engine, serving as prototypes for the Mk XIV. The first teardrop canopy was fitted to a Mk VIII. The T VIII was the prototype two-seat trainer, a conversion made in 1946.

PR VIII

April 1942

Total ordered: **70**

Most of these photo-reconnaissance versions of the Mk VIII went into service as standard and fully armed Mk VIIIs.

MK IX

October 1941–April 1944

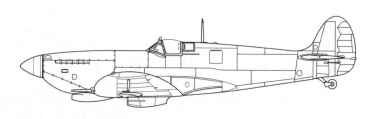

Total built: **5,665**

Wingspan: **36 feet 10 inches**
Length: **31 feet 4 inches**
Empty weight: **5,800 lbs**
Loaded weight: **7,296 lbs**

Engine: **Rolls-Royce Merlin 61, 63, 65A or 66**
Maximum power: **1,475 hp–1,650 hp**
Maximum speed: **408 mph at 25,000 feet**

Service ceiling: **43,000 feet**
Climb to 20,000 feet: **5 minutes 42 seconds**
Rate of climb at 20,000 feet: **3,950 feet per minute**

Typical armament: **four .303 Browning Mk II machine-guns and two 20-mm Hispano cannon**

Mk IXC - Front and top view

Mark Rolfe / Mark Rolfe Technical Art

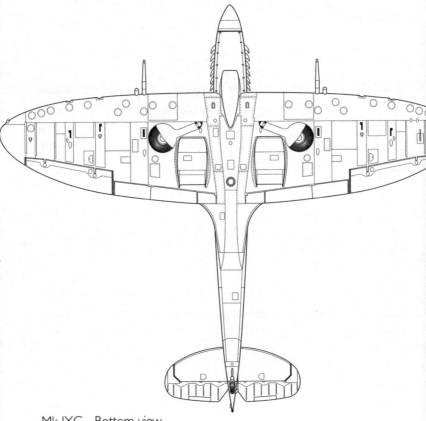

Mk IXC - Bottom view

MK X

May 1942

Total built: **16**

All pressurized Merlin-engined Mk Xs went into service as unarmed PR Xs. A retractable tail-wheel aided streamlining and reduced fuel consumption.

MK XI   *August 1941*

Total built: **464**

This was the PR XI, the RAF's principal photo-reconnaissance Spitfire variant in the later stages of the Second World War. Carefully smoothed airframes allowed a top speed of 417 mph at 24,200 feet. Flight Lieutenant A. F. Martindale dived a PR XI, EN409, at Mach 0.89 on 27 April 1944.

MK XII   *August 1941*

Total built: **100**

The first Griffon-engined Spitfire to enter service with the RAF. Used as low-level interceptor and, with success, against V1 flying bombs. Replaced by the Mk XIV.

MK XIII   *First modifications from Mk VA, August 1942*

Total built: **26**

Low-level armed photo-reconnaissance fighter. Later flew with the Fleet Air Arm.

MK XIV

July 1942–February 1945

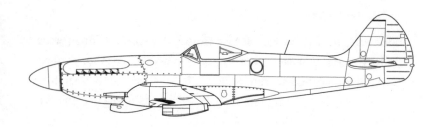

Total built: **957**

Wingspan: **36 feet 10 inches**
Length: **32 feet 8 inches**
Empty weight: **6,376 lbs**
Loaded weight: **8,475 lbs**

Engine: **Rolls-Royce Griffon 65 37-litre liquid-cooled V12**
Maximum power: **2,035 hp**
Maximum speed: **439 mph at 24,500 feet**

Service ceiling: **43,000 feet**
Climb to 20,000 feet: **7 minutes**
Rate of climb at sea level: **4,580 feet per minute**

Typical armament: **four .303 Browning Mk II machine-guns and two 20mm Hispano cannon**

MK XVI   *May 1942*

Total built: **1,053**

Essentially a low-level interceptor version of the Mk IX fitted with Packard-built, 1,580-hp Merlin 266. Some with clipped wings, many with teardrop canopies.

MK XVIII   *December 1942*

Total built: **300**

A souped-up version of the Griffon-powered Mk XIV. Entered service in Far East and India just too late to fight in Second World War. Flown by RAF during Israeli War of Independence, and against communist ground forces during Malayan Emergency, 1951. Maximum speed, 437 mph.

MK XIX   *June 1943*

Total built: **225**

This was the outstanding, unarmed Griffon-engined PR XIX, with a top speed of up to 460 mph, and the last Spitfire mark to be flown with the RAF, until June 1957. Became the basis of RAF's Battle of Britain Memorial Flight. Entered RAF service in May 1945.

F 20

Test flight: April 1942

Total built: **2**

Prototypes for various Griffon-engined marks, especially the F 21.

F 21

March 1942

Total built: **121**

Griffon model with new wing. Development was troubled, giving rise to a widely held Air Ministry opinion that the Spitfire had reached the end of the line. Some were fitted with contra-rotating six-bladed propellers.

F 22

June 1942

Total built: **264**

Successful version of F 21, with teardrop canopy. Entered service with RAF in 1946, and was flown until May 1955. Maximum speed, 449 mph at 25,000 feet. Service ceiling, 45,000 feet.

F 23 *October 1943*

Total built: **I**

Prototype of the Supermarine Valiant, as it was to have been named. The aircraft was a conversion of an F 21. It was to have been armed with six 20-mm cannon. Maiden flight, February 1945.

F 24 *June 1943–November 1945*

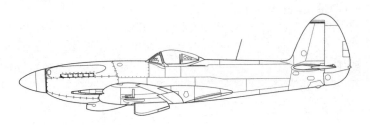

Total built: **78**

Wingspan: **36 feet I I inches**
Length: **32 feet I I inches**
Empty weight: **7,351 lbs**
Loaded weight: **12,150 lbs**

Engine: **Rolls-Royce Griffon 61, 64 or 85**
Maximum power: **2,340 hp**
Maximum speed: **454 mph at 26,000 feet**
Service ceiling: **43,000 feet**

Climb to 20,000 feet: **7 minutes**
Rate of climb at 2,000 feet: **4,100 feet per minute**

Typical armament: **four 20-mm Hispano Mk II or V cannon, plus underwing-mounted rockets**

SEAFIRE

MK IB

In service: June 1942

Total built: **166**

This was the Mk VB converted for work as a carrier-based fighter with the Fleet Air Arm.

MK II

March 1942

Total built: **372**

Conversion from Mk VC, and an altogether more seaworthy fighter than the earlier Mk IB.

MK III

March 1942

Total built: **1,180**

Modification of Mk II with folding wings. In service with Fleet Air Arm until March 1946. Used by French Navy in 1948 to attack communist forces in Indo-China.

MK XV   *March 1943*

Total built: **455**

Griffon-engined variant. Too late to fight in Second World War.

MK XVII   *March 1943*

Total built: **233**

Development of Mk XV with beefed-up airframe, teardrop canopy. In service from late 1945 until November 1954.

MK 45   *August 1944*

Total built: **50**

Carrier-based version of Spitfire F 21. Maximum speed, 450 mph at 19,000 feet. Rate of climb at 4,900 feet, 4,440 feet per minute.

MK 46   *August 1944*

Total built: **25**

A MK 46 with six-bladed contra-rotating propeller and large Spiteful tail. Mainly used as trainer.

MK 47

June 1943–April 1946

Total built: **89**

Production of this fine machine was curtailed by the arrival of naval jets. Range extended to a maximum of 1,250 miles with extra tanks. Fought in Malaya in 1949 and against North Korea in 1950 from HMS *Triumph*. Flew until May 1954.

There are gaps in the numbers of Spitfire marks; this is an omission on Supermarine's part for a number of reasons, including rejected prototypes.

SELECT
BIBLIOGRAPHY

THERE have been, as you might expect, many books published over the years on the Spitfire and especially about those who flew the aircraft in action. Curiously, there are very few in print at any one time, and most have to be hunted down through the second-hand book trade. I cannot begin to remember how many Spitfire books and articles I must have read, and mostly discarded, over the years, but here is a list of those I have read or re-read while writing this book. (Where possible, and helpful, I have provided details of a book's most recent publisher.)

C. F. Andrews and E. B. Morgan, *Supermarine Aircraft Since 1914*, Putnam Aeronautical Books, 1981.

M. J. F. Bowyer, *The Spitfire, 50 Years On*, Patrick Stephens, 1986.

Eric B. Morgan and Edward Shacklady, *Spitfire: The History*, Key Publishing, 1987.

Alfred Price, *The Spitfire Story*, revised 2nd edn, Arms and Armour, 1995.

Alfred Price, *Spitfire: A Complete Fighting History*, Promotional Reprint Co, 1991.

Alfred Price is a Spitfire expert, writing in immense detail and with great authority. His books are not for casual readers but for the dedicated Spitfire and aviation enthusiast. His titles are thoroughly supported by Morgan and Shacklady's encyclopaedic tome which tells you pretty much everything you will ever need to know about the production history of the aircraft. It lists every Spitfire built.

To find out more about the Seafire, try D. Brown, *The Seafire: The Spitfire that Went to Sea*, Greenhill Books, 1986.

R. J. Mitchell is remarkably ill-served by biographers. Someone ought to knuckle down and write a readable and informative biography. Until then we have only a very particular hagiography written by his devoted son: Gordon Mitchell, *R. J. Mitchell, Schooldays to Spitfire*, 3rd edn, Tempus Publishing, 2002.

The Rolls-Royce Heritage Trust is currently researching a comprehensive history of the Merlin engine. Until then, it is worth consulting A. Harvey-Baily, *The Merlin in Perspective: The Combat Years*, Rolls-Royce Heritage Trust, 1983; and B. Gunston, *Rolls-Royce Aero Engines*, Patrick Stephens, 1989.

Two Supermarine test pilots have written their memoirs. Both are enjoyable: Alexander Henshaw, *Sigh for a Merlin: Testing the Spitfire*, new edn, Air Data Publications, 1996; and Jeffrey Quill, *Spitfire: A Test Pilot's Story*, revised edn, Air Data Publications, 1996.

Books on the Battle of Britain have been legion. Some, like Len Deighton's, remain contentious, others, like Bungay's, offer fresh perspectives on this legendary conflict.

Patrick Bishop, *Fighter Boys: Saving Britain 1940*, HarperCollins, 2003.

Stephen Bungay, *The Most Dangerous Enemy*: *A History of the Battle of Britain*, Aurum Press, 2001.

Len Deighton, *Fighter: The True Story of the Battle of Britain* [1977], most recently, Pimlico, 1996.

Peter Townsend, *Duel of Eagles*: *The Struggle for the Skies, 1918–40*, most recently, Phoenix, 2000 (a beautifully written book by one of the most famous British fighter pilots).

Geoffrey Wellum, *First Light*, Penguin, 2003 (a late-flowering masterpiece from a former Spitfire pilot).

To know what it was like to be on the receiving end of a Spitfire at the time, try Ulrich Steinhilper (and Peter Osborne), *Spitfire on My Tail: A View from the Other Side*, 2nd edn, Independent Books, 1990.

There have been many other memoirs by Spitfire pilots. My favourites are:

Pierre Clostermann, *Le Grande Cirque* [*The Big Show*], most recently, in an expanded edition, Weidenfeld and Nicolson, 2004.

Wilfrid Duncan Smith, *Spitfire into Battle* [1981], most recently, John Murray, 2002.

J. E. Johnson, *Full Circle*: *The Story of Air Fighting* [1964], most recently, Cassell Military, 2001 (The RAF's highest-scoring ace takes the story of air combat from the First World War to the jet age, but includes his own extensive experience during the Second World War).

For a taste of Spitfires flying in theatres of war far from the south and east coasts of Britain:

Jim Grant, *Spitfires Over Darwin 1943*, Tech Write Solutions, Melbourne.

Jon Latimer, *Burma, the Forgotten War*, John Murray, 2005.

Christopher Shores, Brian Cull and Nicola Malizia, *Malta: The Spitfire Year, 1942*, Grub Street Publishing, 1991.

For a life of Air Chief Marshal Dowding, try Basil Collier, *Leader of the Few: The Authorised Biography of Air Chief Marshal, the Lord Dowding of Bentley Priory*, Jarrolds, London, 1957; or Peter Brown, *Honour Restored: The Battle of Britain, Dowding, and the Fight for Freedom*, Spellmount, 2004.

For one of Air Chief Marshal Park, see Vincent Orange, *A Biography of Air Chief Marshal Sir Keith Park, GCB, KBE, MC, DFC, DCL*, Methuen, 1984.

And, finally, for an unerring sense of what it was like to be a fighter pilot, albeit one flying Hurricanes over France and Britain or, later, P-40s over the North African desert, try Derek Robinson, *Piece of Cake* and *A Good Clean Fight*, both most recently, Cassell Military, 2003 and 2002 respectively.

INDEX